Laughing at Our Self-Destruction

How to Stop Worrying and Accept the Impending Collapse of Human Civilization

Laughing
at Our
Self-Destruction

How to Stop
Worrying and
Accept
the
Impending
Collapse
of Human
Civilization

Scott Erickson

AZARIA PRESS

CONTENTS

INTRODUCTION – Freedom's just another
word for nothin' left to lose 1

CHAPTER 1 – IS IT ASKING TOO MUCH TO BE ABLE
TO ENJOY A NICE LITTLE RETIREMENT BEFORE
CIVILIZATION COLLAPSES? 13

CHAPTER 2 – DEALING WITH
THE COLLAPSE DENIERS 25

CHAPTER 3 – THE LOVE OF MONEY IS WHAT
KEEPS THE ECONOMY FROM COLLAPSING 49

CHAPTER 4 – RELATABLE REAL-LIFE EFFECTS OF
OUR ADDICTION TO ECONOMIC GROWTH 69

CHAPTER 5 – WHY CAN'T I BUILD A HOME THAT'S
IN HARMONY WITH LIFE? 89

CHAPTER 6 – IF ADDICTION IS A BAD THING, THEN
WHY IS OUR CIVILIZATION DEPENDENT ON IT? 117

CHAPTER 7 – THE OPPOSITE OF LIFE IS
NOT WHAT YOU THINK 145

CHAPTER 8 – IF EVERYBODY IS AGAINST WAR,
THEN WHY DOES IT KEEP HAPPENING? 169

CHAPTER 9 – WHAT ABOUT THE CHILDREN? 193

CHAPTER 10 – CRISIS MANAGEMENT
ON A SINKING SHIP 213

CONCLUSION – How to stop worrying and love
humanity's self-destruction 245

About the Author 259

INTRODUCTION

Freedom's just another
word for nothin' left to lose

We're doomed. By "we" I mean us. All of us. You and me and your favorite movie director and all your friends and the President of the United States and the person who sewed the "do not remove" tag onto your mattress and the person who touches you in the special way that makes you feel tingly all over. We're all doomed.

DOES IT SEEM LIKE THE AUTHOR
ISN'T TAKING THIS SERIOUSLY?

Rest assured, the author takes this very seriously—seriously enough to go through the trouble of writing this book. But just because humanity is doomed, I refuse to let it spoil my day.

Perhaps you're wondering how I was able to get to this point. Perhaps you're asking yourself: How can the author be aware of such a ☹ thing and still be ☺?

ABOUT THE AUTHOR

When I was young (stupid) I believed that it was vitally important to go to the roots, to dig for the solutions to our collective problems and get the answers to humanity as soon as possible. I thought that humanity would be eager for answers. I thought that if someone came up with sensible ideas communicated clearly, humanity would be anxious to apply them in order to create a just, peaceful, sustainable world.

It's so *embarrassing* to write down—to commit to tangible words that could be read by anyone—that I once believed this. Recall that at the time I was young (stupid). But I'm older now, and wiser. The veil of ignorance has been lifted from my eyes. The doors of perception have been cleansed. I've seen infinity in a grain of sand.

Well, maybe not *all* of infinity, but most of it.

Assuming that we want to create a life-affirming civilization— a society based on living in harmony with the principles of life within us and surrounding us, a society focused on achieving peace in all senses of the term, a society that encourages us all to develop our highest potentials, a society that...

Never mind. Things like that require the cultivation of *wisdom.* Remember that word? *No?* I'm not surprised. These days, the word is used only in the context of financial acumen—of the ability to make wise investment choices. In other words, to get rich—to make a profit.

But I'm not interested in that kind of wisdom. The desire to make a profit is pretty much the exact opposite of the kind of wisdom I'm interested in. I don't have any answers that "sell." I'm a prophet with no profit. *(I've been waiting 12 years to use that line.)*

INNOCENCE VERSUS EXPERIENCE

Rather than being eager for the answers, humanity is eager to *avoid* the answers, to distract itself away from the answers, to run away screaming at a mere glimpse of a hint of the answers.

My old self would get outraged over this. My new self delights in the comic absurdity of it. My old self despaired at seeing humanity digging itself deeper into a hole. My new self laughs as humanity says, "Faster, faster! There's light at the end of the tunnel." Well, if humanity wants to think a hole is a tunnel, that's fine by me.

This book is not meant as a call to action, as a proposal for activism of any kind. Because it's too late. Nothing can stop it.

As the song says, "Freedom's just another word for nothin' left to lose." I'm free of having to be serious for the sake of an interested and concerned audience that doesn't exist. They ain't there. I can say anything! I can write grammatically awful sentences like "They ain't there"! I can do whatever want. I can

USE THE SECTION HEADINGS

in wildly inappropriate ways. I can have fun! If it ain't fun, why bother? If nobody else will take humanity's self-destruction seriously, then why should I?

GETTING OUT OF A
CO-DEPENDENT RELATIONSHIP

It's a very strange feeling to give up on the world, to say to the world: *So long, it's been good to know you. Adios. Sayonara. It's been fun, but it's getting late. You'll have to excuse me but I have another engagement.*

I was co-dependent with the world, enabling the world. I was arguing with the world within the framework of the world's assumptions. And as we all know, if you accept the terms of the opponent's argument you've already lost.

But no more! Bye-bye world! I had to explain to the world that I was hoping we could establish a mutually beneficial relationship, but it wasn't working out. I had to tell the world, "Sorry, but there's not enough room in our bed for me, you, and *your issues.*"

WHAT DO YOU MEAN BY
"GIVING UP ON THE WORLD"?

Oh—this is important: By *the world* I'm not referring to the physical aspect of existence, the evolving expression of the universe into more complex forms of stabilized energy. I'm not referring to the interconnected fabric that Buddhism refers to as *Indra's Net*, a beautiful analogy in which every aspect of physical existence is seen as a crystal bead which reflects the entire net—not only the other beads but also the other reflections—creating endless images of a shimmering, undivided whole.

No, that part's pretty cool.

What I mean by *the world*—the world I've given up on—is the *human* world: the world that humanity has created by shaping the physical world, by rearranging its materials, by channeling its energies. Because humanity has shaped the world based on underlying assumptions that are fundamentally wrong and are the cause of our impending self-destruction.

BUT CAN'T WE FIX EVERYTHING BY VOTING FOR SOMEONE DIFFERENT IN THE NEXT ELECTION?

Hahaha! I'll get to you later.

ARE WE REALLY DOOMED?

That's an excellent question, which the remainder of this book will answer. *Spoiler Alert: The answer is YES.* Some people agree with this, while other people are deluded fools. To explore this further, let's create a new section with a heading as it might be written by somebody with one of those old-fashioned flip phones. Remember those? They didn't have a keyboard, so you had to press the number keys to make letters. This took FOREVER. So to save time, the section heading might be written like this:

WHICH SIDE R U ON?

When the question of humanity's impending self-destruction comes up, people generally divide themselves up into two sides—two "teams" if you will.

The first side—Team Denial—is shocked at the idea. The second side—Team Truth—is shocked that the first side is shocked. "How can you possibly be shocked?" they say. "Don't you watch the news?"

By the way, the Surgeon General has declared that watching the news is hazardous to mental health and is a leading cause of indigestion and high blood pressure.

I'm pleased to report that the views of Team Truth are rising in popularity. Collapse-orientated websites and online discussion groups are increasing. More people are watching apocalyptic movies and thinking they're watching documentaries. More people are watching the news and thinking they're watching an apocalyptic movie.

So the truth is spreading! The "We're Doomed!" side is winning! Yay!

WHY ARE YOU READING THIS THING?

I wonder, gentle reader, what brought you here to this book. Perhaps you're here because you've come to suspect the truth of my thesis—the whole "we're doomed" thing. And it would soothe your troubled mind to receive validation. Perhaps you're beginning to suspect that you're going crazy—that you're losing your marbles, that you're playing solitaire without a full deck. Or in other words, that you're a few bricks shy of a full load.

In that case, I'm here to assure you that you have a complete set of marbles, cards, and bricks. You're not insane. You're also kind of cute, when the light hits you just right. And you're very interesting when I've been drinking whiskey sours.

WHY DID I WRITE THIS THING?

I wrote this book as a way to say a final "farewell" to the human race. But more importantly, I wrote this book in hopes of reaching people that also want to understand. Perhaps I can be the person I wish would have written to me when I suspected that I wasn't firing on all cylinders.

Being sane in an insane world is bound to make anybody feel crazy. But I've come to believe that what makes us crazy isn't so much what we're going through as the feeling that we're going through it alone—that nobody on earth can relate to what we're going through.

The other thing that can drive us crazy is not understanding *why*—not understanding the reasons for why things are the way they are. We can deal with quite a bit if we understand the reasons for it.

IT'S ALL ABOUT YOU

By the end of this book, you will understand why everything is going to hell. You will understand why humanity is goin' down... down... down... You will understand the reasons for environmental destruction, for the impending economic collapse, for the rising cost of living, for fundamentalism, war, political dysfunction, and the resurgence of fascist impulses including... *wait for it*... the election of Donald Trump!

What about bad fashion choices? Sorry, this book will *not* help you understand the reasons for bad fashion choices. Honestly, I've put almost no thought into that problem. But perhaps future thinkers can work on that one. I don't want to use up all the thinking. Leave some room for other people to think, I always say.

HERE'S A FUN LITTLE IDEA...

...although perhaps bound to be a bit "controversial" to some people. Here's the fun little idea:

WE'RE GETTING EXACTLY
WHAT WE DESERVE

To some degree (a very large degree) our problems are created and sustained by the nation's ruling classes, whose wealth and power give them the ability to insulate themselves from those problems. And there's no way they're going to change unless they're forced to.

If only we had a government in which people had a say in how they were governed. Wouldn't that be great? Because we could figure out better ways to do things, then impel our government to do them. We could rally behind the words of Gandhi: "When the people lead, the leaders will follow." And any leaders who didn't follow would be out of a job. You might say that such a government would be "by the people and for the people."

Wait a minute... There's a name for that kind of government. It's called a *democracy!* And it's exactly the kind of government we have! And in a democracy we get what we ask for, or are stuck with what we passively accept. Of course, we'd have to be smart enough to figure out better ways to do things. Along those lines, here's another possibly controversial little idea:

HUMANITY IS DUMB

This idea might not be controversial to you, personally, because you interpret it as "everybody else is dumb." But how smart are you, *really?* Can you answer these questions?

1. Who's buried in Grant's tomb?

2. How much wood could a woodchuck chuck?

3. What's the name of a woman with no arms and no legs in the middle of a tennis court?

The answers are at the end of this chapter.

Also, if you're so smart then what do you think we should do about the fact that our economy is based on a pyramid scheme?

OUR ECONOMY IS BASED ON A PYRAMID SCHEME?

Perhaps you're beginning to suspect that this author is some sort of "conspiracy nut" who wears a tinfoil cap to insulate his brain from transmissions from the mothership?

That's not the case at all. The tinfoil cap is a fashion statement.

A recent article bears me out. I should point out that the article was *not* published in a pamphlet put out by some guy living in a trailer park in Idaho. It was published by *Forbes*—a legitimate and well-respected publication, although not as fun as the pamphlet put out by the guy in Idaho. The title of the article is: "The World Economy is a Pyramid Scheme, Steven Chu Says."

Who's Steven Chu? He's an American physicist and Nobel laureate, and was the 12th United States Secretary of Energy. He's currently the William R. Kenan, Jr., Professor of Physics and Professor of Molecular and Cellular Physiology at Stanford University. In other words, he's a really smart dude, although not as fun as the guy in Idaho.

Here's an interesting question: Why wasn't this a major news story? You'd think the issue would be considered to be important, because one problem with pyramid schemes is their tendency to collapse. Which is something that—if it happened to our economy—would have results that could be labelled as "not good."

Many other smart people have concluded that our economy is based on a pyramid scheme, as we'll explore later. We'll also explore later why there's not a chance in hell that any mainstream economist is going to publicly admit that our economy is based on a pyramid scheme. At least, not any mainstream economist that wants to keep their job as a mainstream economist.

Perhaps we might want to consider changing the economy so it's *not* based on a pyramid scheme? Maybe I'm crazy, but wouldn't that be a good idea? Speaking of crazy ideas, here's one of the craziest ideas I've ever heard:

HUMANITY IS THE
PINNACLE OF EVOLUTION

Hahaha! Seriously? A species that made the movie *Beverly Hills Chihuahua* is the pinnacle of evolution? A species that created the

Jackie Chan's Nose Shower Shampoo Dispenser is the pinnacle of evolution?

Yes, the *Jackie Chan's Nose Shower Shampoo Dispenser* is an actual product. There's no way I could make that up. How does it work? Well, according to the description on Amazon.com, "Just press the nose, and gel oozes out of the right nostril." *Only 16 left in stock - order soon!*

Why is it that some people think of humanity as the pinnacle of evolution? (The question doesn't apply to those who believe that the God-being plopped us into existence a few thousand years ago, along with all the dinosaur fossils to "test our faith" or whatever the excuse is these days.)

I imagine that many (or most) people would offer an answer along the lines of: "Oh, that's a no-brainer! We're the pinnacle of evolution because we dominate the earth and turn all the materials and processes of life to our own advantage."

So... We're the pinnacle of evolution because we level forests and use the wood to build Chick-fil-A franchises. And we turn grasslands into factory farms for antibiotic-filled chickens to make into the surprisingly delicious Chick-n-Minis.

"Exactly!" replies many (or most) people. Although some conclude that humanity's status as the pinnacle of evolution is assured by the Burger King Bacon and Cheese Whopper.

This author would like to advance the proposition that the reasoning "because we dominate the earth and turn all the materials and processes of life to our own advantage" is not proof that we're the pinnacle of evolution. This author would like to advance the proposition that this reasoning is proof of something like the exact opposite.

WE'RE SPECIAL, AREN'T WE?

But surely there's something "special" about humanity? Surely we exhibit qualities that put us on a higher level than slime mold and those beetles who stick their butts in the air and squirt stinky stuff at us. Surely humanity isn't *inferior* to the rest of life—or even worse, a freak; an evolutionary mistake.

No, I'm *not* claiming that humanity is a mistake. But I *do* claim that it's possible for humanity to embrace some mistaken ideas. And I acknowledge that there's something special about humanity, although I think it has nothing to do with Chick-n-Minis or the Bacon and Cheese Whopper. More on that later.

A LITTLE "P.S." TO THE ABOVE ↑

The evolution-believers claim that humanity is superior because we dominate the earth and turn all the materials and processes of life to our own advantage. Curiously, the people who *don't* accept the concept of evolution—who believe that the God-being plopped us into existence a few thousand years ago—believe that humanity is superior *for exactly the same reason.* Or as the God-being dictated to someone who knew how to write, "Be fruitful and multiply and fill the earth and subdue it, and have dominion over the fish of the sea and over the birds of the heavens and over every living thing that moves on the earth."

Interesting... The evolution-believers and the God-being-believers disagree on so much. But on this one particular thing they drink in solidarity and give each other high-fives and chest bumps.

EMBRACING CONTRADICTION

I recently spent six glorious days in Anza-Borrego State Park in the Colorado Desert in extreme Southern California. Absolutely beautiful! Some of the most amazing desert scenery I've ever experienced.

Within the park is a small town, Borrego Springs, which has many great qualities. It's an official Dark Sky Community, so at night residents are able to see the abundant stars and ponder the amazing evolving universe of which we are an integral part. Borrego Springs also supports the arts, with the town surrounded by hundreds of whimsical sculptures of horses, dragons, and other real and mythical creatures.

SOUNDS LIKE A NICE LITTLE TOWN

It is! However, in the town I found a sign with the heading "Borrego Water District – WATER FACTS" which explained that Borrego Springs is using water 70 percent faster than "natural recharge." According to the sign, "This is called an OVERDRAFT and just like your bank account, we cannot continue without consequences."

Oh no! ☹ But the situation isn't hopeless. ☺

The sign concluded with the following message: "The District is working with the Borrego Water Coalition, the County of San Diego, and the State of California to address this important issue."

Yes, the great little universe-positive, art-supporting town is unsustainable. Just like our culture! You might even say that the great little town is a microcosm of our culture.

Actually, you don't have to say it because I just wrote it.

Borrego Springs is running out of water, and is hoping for some larger entity to bring it more water. The problem is, the rest of the world is also running out of water. And there's no larger entity beyond the world that we can appeal to for more water.

Oops!

Existence is amazing, beautiful, sublime—an utter and complete miracle. And the human ability to comprehend this is another miracle. Also, humanity is doing the best it can to destroy the miracle. Actually, to destroy both miracles. Because they're connected: You can't destroy the first miracle without destroying the second miracle.

WHAT'S THE POINT, AUTHOR?

The point is: We don't need to limit ourselves to accepting either the positive or negative, the affirmation of life or the destruction of life. Our minds are capable of expanding enough to encompass both.

Our civilization appreciates the miracle enough to preserve small bits of it. It acknowledges that in some places the miracle should be allowed to exist without our interference. And outside those preserves, our civilization continually destroys the miracle in order to extract whatever's necessary to keep our doomed civilization going for a little longer.

Answers to the questions from earlier in this chapter:

1. *Hard to tell, it's just a bunch of bones in there*

2. *As much as it feels like chucking*

3. *Annette*

CHAPTER 1

IS IT ASKING TOO MUCH TO BE ABLE TO ENJOY A NICE LITTLE RETIREMENT BEFORE CIVILIZATION COLLAPSES?

This author recently became retired, and is hoping to enjoy a nice little retirement before everything blows up. Is that too much to ask for? I'm not sure how much time is left before the ship goes down for good. The collapse is well underway, and it's happening right on my street. Within five blocks of where I live, at least a dozen people are living in their vehicles. The garbage area where I live continues to be raided. And I live in one of the better neighborhoods, in one of the better cities.

Some people think America is the greatest nation on earth. But the number of people who think this is declining steadily. More people are questioning the greatness of a country in which an increasing proportion of the population is living in their vehicles and stealing garbage.

America is going down. Humanity is going down. But I'm determined to have a nice little retirement before the ship sinks.

NO, THE AUTHOR ISN'T RICH

How can I afford to be retired? At this point—with wages dropping and the cost of living rising—few people can even think about retirement. Most people have resigned themselves to the idea that their "golden years" will consist of wearing a paper hat and serving Happy Meals. So how did this author, an extremely non-rich person, manage to become retired? Well, since I'm such a nice guy, here's some retirement advice!

HOW TO RETIRE FOR SUPER-CHEAP

Not too many years ago, your thoughtful and devoted author (me) was unemployed and heavily in debt. Your thoughtful and devoted author (me again) was seriously considering the option of cashing out a bunch of credit cards, moving far away, and living in the back of a truck under an assumed identity.

Climbing out of this hole involved some tough decisions, a lot of work, and a couple of lucky breaks. One of those lucky breaks was getting a somewhat decent job that, for 15 years, gave me a reliable income at the level of "upper lower class."

But with such a humble income, how on God's green earth did I get to the point where a nice little retirement was possible? Probably the most important advice I can offer is to adopt the philosophy: "Living simply is a cheap way to be rich." This isn't idealistic nonsense. It's a change in attitude that can result in lots of practical strategies.

As far as how to retire without being rich, many of those strategies are outlined in a book I frequently recommend: *How to Retire the Cheapskate Way: The Ultimate Cheapskate's Guide to a Better, Earlier, Happier Retirement*, by Jeff Yeager. Rather than try to save a ton of money so you can retire with a "normal" (expensive) lifestyle, the idea is to create a lifestyle that doesn't require a ton of money.

HOW TO TRAVEL FOR SUPER-CHEAP

One application of the above: I love to travel. For me, travel mostly translates to backpacking and car camping. Both of these can cost very little money.

While backpacking, I've camped in places with better views than the finest motels in the world, for *free*. I've done several major car camping road trips. The longest one was for six months, and it cost less than what I'd been spending for rent, utilities, and all the other expenses required for a "normal" lifestyle. By living frugally, I had the opportunity to enjoy half a year of amazing experiences visiting some of the most incredible places on earth, for only a few thousand dollars.

Do you "need" an expensive motel so you can shower in luxury? Or would you be willing to take a shower in a mountain meadow with a bucket of water and a bar of soap? Would you consider that to be a sacrifice? Or would you consider it to be a positive experience that makes you feel part of the wondrous fabric of life on this planet? Yeah, maybe you'd end up with a few mosquito bites, but c'mon...

RETIREMENT ADVICE FOR TODAY'S YOUNG PEOPLE

I feel very bad for today's young people. Most of them don't need to be convinced that our civilization is on a downward slide toward collapse. They're expecting it. They're also expecting that they'll need to work until their knees give out. Most young people of today have added *retirement* to their list of *Things I'll Never Achieve*, along with climbing Mt. Everest and owning their own home.

And if today's young people complain about any of this, the previous generation—today's not-so-young people—call today's young people a bunch of whiners whose problems are caused by blowing their money on avocado toast.

As an older obsolete person, I have some advice for younger obsolete persons. I've been barely able to squeak out a frugal (cheap) retirement just before I became unmarketable—before my brand became obsolete. Just for the record, my brand currently consists of "I have a metabolism." Which isn't very marketable, but on the positive side it's good for my health.

I'm very fortunate to have been able to achieve a cheapskate retirement. But the way things are going (downhill, rapidly) even a cheapskate retirement is becoming increasingly difficult to afford. So for young people of today to have a nice little retirement, desperate measures are necessary.

USEFUL ADVICE IS ON
THE WAY, EVENTUALLY

But first, let's conduct an honest assessment of your situation. As for you, young people of today, as far as retirement possibilities go, you're screwed. It took me most of my life to become obsolete. You, however, were essentially *born* obsolete. Any education you receive—any skill you master—will soon (if it hasn't since you started reading this) be rendered obsolete by AI and robotics. If you're not in the process of becoming obsolete, then your job consists of working to make *other people* obsolete—as someone else is working to make *you* obsolete. And on and on, until the final person joins the rest of us in submissive worship of our robot overlords.

Financial experts, whose advice has resulted in suicidal depression for everyone they've given it to, say that in order to retire comfortably you need to save, at minimum, seven hundred thousand billion dollars. And your job—if you're lucky enough to have one—pays minimum wage plus 50 cents. Why do they bother with that worthless 50 cents? It's so your employer can feel generous and justify that the CEO makes two million dollars per year because, hey, at least they're not so cruel as to make you get by on minimum wage.

Sure, maybe you could cut down on the avocado toast and scrape together enough nickels to put into a 401k, except that we all know it's only a matter of time—and not much time—before the economy collapses, *really* collapses, in a way that will make all the billionaires who saw it coming (because they helped create it) hop into their private jets and head to their escape properties in New Zealand.

So you're thinking, probably correctly, that investing in avocado toast is much better option, since it gives a tangible and satisfying Return on Investment. Much better than throwing your money into a toilet and waiting for somebody to flush it.

AN ESCAPE PROPERTY
FOR THE REST OF US

Maybe you don't want to just sit around eating avocado toast and waiting for the zombie apocalypse. Maybe you have an idea to escape the upcoming collapse, just like those billionaires. But you can't afford a luxurious escape property stocked with canned caviar and freeze-dried *foie gras*. But perhaps you could scrape together enough nickels for a shack in the forest filled with cans of beans?

Sorry, but it's not possible to buy canned avocado toast.

Just imagine... There you are, deciding whether dinner will consist of kidney beans or garbanzos, eyeballing the surrounding trees with your trusty AK-47 locked and loaded, mumbling *Go ahead, make my day* to the squirrel that's making threatening chirping sounds and scurrying closer to your beans. Maybe that squirrel is a drug addict? Maybe it's a nuclear-powered robot squirrel sent by the government? Maybe it's a genetically-altered mutant squirrel that has stainless steel can-opener teeth? Maybe you're losing your mind? *Go ahead, make my day*.

NON-STANDARD WAYS TO
SAVE ENOUGH MONEY TO RETIRE

Let's re-visit the advice of the financial experts, who told you that to retire you'll need to save as much money as you'll earn in 27 lifetimes. This is not as unrealistic as it may seem. Do you believe in past lives? If you saved all your money during your previous 26 lifetimes, then in this lifetime you should be all set. Except that during your last lifetime you blew it all in Vegas.

Don't worry, there's another option. Maybe you can go back in time to 1763, deposit 14 cents in an interest-bearing savings account, then come back to the present and withdraw enough money to retire. If you can't afford a time machine right now, that's okay. You'll just need to save everything you earn for the next 400 years.

MONEY ISN'T EVERYTHING

After the financial experts have set up an impossible expectation, they'll tell you that the money you'll never have isn't enough to have a *meaningful* retirement. They tell you not to think of retirement as an escape *from* something (a meaningless low-paying job). They'll tell to think of retirement as an opportunity to *achieve* something. You need something to go *toward*—a vision of a lifestyle that will spark joy, that will make your spirit soar, that will resonate with your so-called "soul" as if you had such a thing.

You have a vision? For goodness sake, let us know what it is!

Oh, that sounds delightful! You envision yourself on your luxurious yacht, floating peacefully on the azure seas of the Mediterranean, watching the setting sun cast a warm glow onto the surrounding hills. And there, atop the highest hill, you catch a glimpse of your hillside mansion resplendent in white marble with gold trim. And as you enjoy the view, you are surrounded by servants peeling grapes and placing them gently into your mouth as they touch you in ways that make you glad to be alive.

But is that what you *really* want? Consider how boring that would be: a life of nothing but pointless leisure, of doing nothing productive, of not contributing to the betterment of life or devoting your energies to something greater than yourself. Surely you'll agree that this is a meaningless vision. Also, you can't afford it.

Don't set yourself up for failure. Keep your expectations realistic. Consider retirement visions within your budget. Desires can be met in ways that don't necessarily require a personal income equal to the GNP of Lithuania.

Perhaps you rate *frequent travel to exotic locations* highly on your retirement bucket list? Envision yourself pushing your shopping cart to exotic neighborhoods on the other side of town, visiting dumpsters you've never dumpstered before. Envision yourself excitedly opening the lid, wondering what new treasures await. You're momentarily disappointed at seeing nothing other than a can of peaches in syrup. Gross! *But wait...*

What's that thing under the can of peaches? Could it be? Yes, it is! It's a severed arm! Which would be delicious grilled over a riverside campfire and seasoned with that expired bottle of ketchup you dumpstered yesterday. As long as you can keep the raccoons from stealing it before it's done.

What's that you say? This vision doesn't spark joy?

IT'S ALL ABOUT LOVE

Here's some retirement advice you might have heard: "Do what you love for a living, and you'll never have to work a day in your life." Thus, the entire concept of "retirement" is obsolete. You won't want to retire if you love your work. Which is good advice, since you'll never be able to afford to not work. This is very similar to the advice: "If you love your job, you'll never want to take a vacation." Which is good advice, since you'll never be able to afford a vacation.

What do you love to do? Maybe what you love to do is hanging out with your friends. Well, you might find it challenging to find someone to pay you for that. So once again we need to be *realistic*—to align what you love with actual employment opportunities that pay in something other than good vibes.

So you'll have to learn to love driving an Amazon delivery truck with a pee jug because they don't give enough time for bathroom stops. Or stocking shelves at Safeway, and loving how your manager yells, "I want to see more hustle in your bustle!" And then loving how, if you ask your manager, "What's that supposed to mean?" receiving the reply, "Get the hell back to work!"

Basically, the idea is to love a job in which you're humiliated on a daily basis. This option is especially good for masochists, because you can make the desire to be humiliated work *for* you. Instead of paying a dominatrix to humiliate you, an employer will pay you to be humiliated. Business and pleasure aligned! A win-win situation for everybody!

BUT I'M NOT A MASOCHIST!

If you're unable to get into the whole masochism thing, there's always the option of denial—very popular in America, especially these days. You can be like my former co-worker Nathaniel, whom I worked with until the final thing I was qualified to do became obsolete. Nathaniel was a rising star in the department, admired for his brand of "Person who will continue to attempt to meet expectations that will be ten percent more than whatever I do no matter how hard I work."

Nathaniel hated his job, which was meaningless and required humiliating himself on a daily basis. But, as with all of us, he was forced to take the job to afford to not starve. *Hate job... Need job... Hate job... Need job...*

How to deal with this cognitive dissonance, which could drive a sensitive and self-aware person insane? The problem is obviously being sensitive and self-aware, so let's nip the problem in the bud. I shall never forget what Nathaniel said to me, while staring at his computer screen and typing away like a madman, with stress in his voice and a pained expression on his face: "I love my job."

Yay! Score another win for denial! Sorry, sensitivity and self-awareness, better luck next time.

BRANDING IS STUPID

The whole thing is so dehumanizing—this idea of needing to brand ourselves as products to be sold like socks, or like odor-eating shoe insoles for people who don't wash those socks often enough.

What if we could discuss this with George Washington and Thomas Jefferson? Could you imagine what they'd say if we brought them forward in time, and explained that they founded a country in which personal success depended on having a marketable brand?

Maybe Washington would have been okay with the idea, since he did pretty well with his brand of "Father of our country." But

Jefferson probably would have been dismayed by the idea, due to the negative feedback regarding his brand of "Father of a child with one of his slaves."

MY BRAND IS YOUR BRAND

To be the one who gets hired—the one that stands out amongst the other applicants—it's important that our brand is aligned with the company's brand. If we're interviewing for a job at McDonalds, and we're told that we need to be available for any shift on any day between 5:00am and 11:00pm with one hour's notice, we need to reply "I'm lovin' it!" A much better catchphrase, more closely aligned with employee attitudes and actual customer experience, would be "I'm toleratin' it!" But extensive marketing research determined that this catchphrase would cause customers to go to Burger King, with its catchphrase "At least we're not McDonalds."

But if you have your heart set on McDonalds, you're stuck with "I'm Lovin' It!" which at least sums up your feelings about getting paid. The truth, of course, would be something like "I'm willing to destroy any remaining self-respect to avoid living on the street." But that doesn't demonstrate the sort of "can-do" attitude that will keep Ronald McDonald happy. And if you thought that happy Ronald McDonald was creepy, pray that your eyes will never gaze upon the soul-melting terror that is angry Ronald McDonald. The only thing creepier than angry Ronald McDonald, of course, is horny Ronald McDonald.

UNREQUITED LOVE

Which reminds me of one aspect of the brand that all employees are required to pretend to have: "I love my company." Or if not explicitly required to *love* their company, they're required to occasionally make out with their company in the backseat of a car. Hopefully a cool car like a 1957 Chevy Bel-Air at a drive-in theater watching *Horror at Party Beach* while your company hopes that you'll let them touch you underneath your sweater.

Interestingly, some employees take the whole *branding* thing very seriously, and get tattoos of the company logo. Yes, such employees permanently alter their bodies to identify themselves as part of a company that's doing everything it can to outsource them or replace them with a computer program. If you're one of these people, keep in mind that *branding* is something done to cattle to mark them as property of the ranch. This is very important for the ranch, so they get reimbursed for the meat when the cattle are sent to the slaughterhouse. And another thing—which guys might want to keep in mind—is that this branding is done at around the same time that male cows are castrated.

Okay, young people of today. That concludes our honest assessment of your situation. Now we can proceed to the useful advice.

USEFUL ADVICE!

If the previous visions failed to spark joy, here's some advice that might spark some joy for you. This advice will not only allow you to achieve the retirement you thought you'd never have, but it might also allow you to own the home you thought you'd never be able to afford.

You're pissed-off at your parents, right? You should be! Because it's all their fault; it's 100 percent their fault. You have no fault; it's 0 percent your fault. Why? *Because you didn't ask to be born.* They decided to give birth to you. But did you want to be born? Did they even ask?

They brought you into this deteriorating world and, 18 years later, told you "Good luck, kid" then slapped a *We're Spending Our Child's Inheritance* bumper sticker on their RV and drove off to spend the winter drinking Vodka Gimlets in Orlando and trying to not fall off the golf cart. And then they have the nerve to tell you to plan for retirement by investing responsibly with the money you'll never have.

Do you want to know how to achieve a comfortable retirement while wiping that smug "We're spending the winter getting drunk in Florida" smile off your parent's faces?

Sue them! That's right, sue your parents. Sue their pants off. And their shirts. And their RV. Sure, when you were 14 years old and shouted, in your snarkiest attitude, "I didn't ask to be born!" they laughed it off. But will they laugh when you express this is in a lawsuit?

CONSENT IS IMPORTANT

Since you didn't consent to be born, you can sue for damages. Since you didn't consent to be brought into existence, you can sue your parents for all expenses incurred to sustain your continued existence throughout the course thereof, which is how it will be stated on the legal documents. Lawyers are your friend. Revenge is a dish best served by process servers.

It's your parents fault. It was *their* decision to get together and do the nasty thing to create you—to make a zygote that would grow for nine months before mom squeezed you out, unfinished by the way, before you were ready, *without receiving consent*.

As we all know, consent is important. Not just ethically, but legally. For example, let's say somebody strips off your clothes, ties you to a bed, and forces you to watch the entire final season of *Two and a Half Men*. If you gave consent to that—and if you did, why the hell did you consent to that?—then everything's cool. But what if you did *not* give consent? In that case, *bring on the lawyers!*

All the evidence is on your side. There's a birth certificate that clearly lays the blame where it belongs. If there's a document that proves you agreed to this travesty of justice, let them produce it. *Go ahead, make my day.*

MY LAWYER SAID I HAD
TO ADD THIS STATEMENT

DISCLAIMER: I'm not actually qualified to give legal advice, because I'm not actually a lawyer. But I know a little about legal stuff because one time I talked with a guy at a bar who saw a movie that had an actor playing a lawyer. Or maybe it was a cop? I can't remember, I was drinking at the time.

DO YOU LIKE WHISKEY?

Perhaps, young people of today, the strategy of *Sue Your Parents* will work for some of you. If so, then you can join me in having a nice little retirement before everything blows up. On that note, I'd like to make a deal with you.

When it happens, if I'm still alive and kicking, my plan is to watch from the top of a local hillside with a bottle of Makers. But I might not be very mobile at that point—I might be using a walker or wheelchair. If so, I'll need some help reaching the summit. If you help me, I'll share my Makers. We can make a final toast to humanity, and have a good laugh about how absolutely hilarious it is that so many people refused to believe that the collapse was coming.

CHAPTER 2

DEALING WITH THE
COLLAPSE DENIERS

Perhaps you don't agree with the author's belief that we're doomed? Perhaps you wish to argue vehemently with the author? (If you're not familiar with the word *vehemently*, it means "while holding a slab of bacon.")

Perhaps you recall an instance of a doomsday prophet predicting The End will come on Thursday. Then on Friday they explained that they meant *next* Thursday. Then next Friday you saw the doomsday prophet working at Wendy's. When you asked them about The End, they replied, "Would you like fries with that?"

But you know what? Sometimes doomsday prophets are right. For example, just a few months before the Fall of Rome a fish peddler named Ignatius Targus walked around with a sign proclaiming THE END IS NEAR. City officials laughed at him, then ordered him to be thrown to the lions. So Ignatius Targus was correct, for Rome as well as for Ignatius Targus.

Here's a more recent example. It happened the other night at Darwin's Theory—my neighborhood pub, the place where "everybody knows your name" unless they had too many shots of Jim Beam. What happened is that Mark declared the prophecy that he would drink too much and not be able to drive home. Then, John declared the prophecy that he would not get laid that night. BOTH PROPHECIES CAME TO BE.

But I suppose those prophecies aren't terribly important compared to prophecies about collapsing civilizations. Some people might—

Hold on, some random guy just showed up. And it looks like he's in a mood to argue vehemently.

Hello, random guy. Do you disagree with the notion that our civilization is on the verge of collapse?

"I concede that *some* civilizations collapse. But that could never happen to *our* civilization."

Why not?

"Because it hasn't happened yet."

And therefore it can't happen?

"Yes! Exactly!"

I must tell you, gentle reader, that such reasoning is an excellent example of why our collapse is immanent. If members of a civilization believe that collapse is impossible, they will misinterpret all the signs that their civilization is collapsing. We become like the captain of the *Titanic*, who believed that the ship was unsinkable. As the ship was going down, he told the crew, "We're not sinking. It's just the ship doing an impression of a submarine."

MONEY AS INSULATION

A variety of worsening problems clearly indicate that we're doomed. If you aren't experiencing those problems, it's probably because you have a lot of money. There are many wonderful things about money, and one of them is that money can insulate you from society's problems.

If you have enough money, you don't have to live in a slum or in one of America's various "cancer alleys." You can afford to live in a neighborhood where you'll never encounter a rat gnawing on a homeless person that's rummaging through a dumpster being spray-painted by taggers while fentanyl addicts set themselves on fire. You can afford to insulate yourself from problems such as homeless people trying to steal your garbage. As opposed to homeless people, who have become one of the problems and can't afford to insulate themselves from themselves.

If you have *lots* of money, you can afford to live in a gated community with a perimeter wall that will prevent you from seeing any problems. And with enough money, that gated community can afford to hire armed guards who will shoot any problems that try to get in.

But what about *you?* You're not rich. But you can experience what it's like to be rich for a few days. All you have to do is scrape together enough nickels to afford a visit to *Tourist Town*.

TOURIST TOWN

Tourist Town can afford to do things that aren't within the budget of the place where you live. That's because Tourist Town makes lots of money from people like you, who want to temporarily escape the problems they can't afford to insulate themselves from at home.

At Tourist Town, you won't have your delicate sensibilities offended by the sight of graffiti, because Tourist Town can afford to pay people to remove graffiti every single morning. Same thing with garbage, because early every morning—long before you drag your lazy ass out of bed—employees of Tourist Town are actively removing trash and scraping chewing gum off the sidewalks.

Another thing you won't see on the sidewalks is homeless people. Because if someone like that manages to show up, an employee from Tourist Town responds quickly to offer compassionate assistance in the form of a one-way bus ticket to the place where you live.

If you think that the residents of Tourist Town are treating you nicely only because of your money, that's a sign that you think too much. The important thing is to keep the money flowing. Just like the quaint stream that flows peacefully through the heart of Tourist Town. Which is best viewed from the patio of the fancy wine bar where the menu doesn't list prices, allowing you to experience the lifestyle of people for whom money is no object. While the stream and your money are flowing, all of society's problems are gone. Just don't let your money run out, because it will mean that—from the perspective of Tourist Town—*you* have become one of the problems.

Sure, it'll cost you. But isn't it nice to pretend to be rich, just for a couple of days? You can demand excellent service from people that aren't allowed to tell customers "no." In other words, you can play the role of an entitled jerk, if only for a few glorious days of relief from having to pretend to be considerate of the needs of other people.

Unfortunately, the good times can't last forever. Sooner than you had hoped, your credit cards are maxed out and it's time to bid a fond farewell to Tourist Town. It's time to go home, where you'll have to deal with the things that you could temporarily pretend didn't exist. Such as that homeless person who just got off the bus and is rummaging through your garbage. But wasn't it nice to pretend, just for a little while?

A MONEY-MAKING SCHEME

In the previous chapter, this author explained some of his strategies for how to travel for super-cheap. But it's nice to splurge every now and then, right? I'm about ready for a trip to Tourist Town. But I'm broke. What should I do to make some money? Sell blood plasma? Take a part-time job as a male escort?

Here's a money-making scheme I've used on occasion. I know a way to get people to send you money for nothing in return. Do you want to know how to do it? To find out, send ten dollars to this author.

ANOTHER MONEY-MAKING SCHEME

Product Placement! They do it all the time in movies to make a little extra money. So why not in books? But don't worry, gentle reader, I vow to mention only quality products in ways that are relevant to whatever important points that I'm trying to make. For example, to cut through lies and obfuscations in search of truth and to assist in quality hair styling, this author recommends the Suvorna Ador 6.5-inch thinning scissors. Suvorna isn't the cheapest brand, but the superior quality and durability make it a bargain in the long run.

COLLAPSE IS AN EXCELLENT BOOK
WHICH THIS AUTHOR ENDORSES

The book is was written by Jared Diamond, who is much smarter than you. The full title of the book is, *Collapse: How Societies Choose to Fail or Succeed*. I would have been happy to plug Jared Diamond's book in exchange for money. But when I suggested this he pretended to be working at Pizza Hut and asked if I wanted extra cheese. So I'm plugging his book for the old-fashioned reason that it's simply a darn good book. It provides an abundance of historical examples and scientific research to support its conclusions, and it has pictures. None of the pictures are of naked people, so if that's what you're looking for I would recommend another book.

If you're still reading at this point, and aren't searching for books with pictures of naked people, perhaps you're interested in the question of why civilizations collapse. Perhaps you're curious whether there's an answer to the question: *Is there, perhaps, a single overriding cause that's common to all the civilizations examined in the book?*

The answer is: *Yes, there is!*

The single overriding cause that's common to all the civilizations examined in the book is: *Poor grooming habits.*

Just kidding! *Poor grooming habits* is only a secondary cause.

The primary cause is: *Environmental destruction*. It's true! Past civilizations have collapsed for refusing to recycle their coffee cozies. Also, for some other things. In the introduction to *Collapse*, Diamond writes:

> The processes through which past societies have undermined themselves fall into eight categories, whose relative importance differs from case to case: deforestation and habitat destruction, soil problems (erosion, salinization, and fertility losses), water management problems, overhunting, overfishing, effects of introduced species on native species, human population growth, and increased per-capita impact of people.

Jared Diamond's central thesis is thoroughly convincing. Many prominent academic-types have tried to disprove it, but in all cases Jared Diamond has prevailed. In one case, an angry college professor lunged at Jared Diamond with a sword, but Jared Diamond overcame the assailant with a pen. So I guess it's true what they say.

DEFYING NATURE DEFIES US?

I believe it was Chief Seattle who said, "We are but one strand within the web of life. Whatever we do to the web comes back to bite us in the ass." And there's the oft-quoted line by Ralph Waldo Emerson: "Drive out nature with a pitchfork, she comes running back with a shotgun."

These words of wisdom confirm the idea that defying nature defies us. Which implies that preserving the environment is a good thing.

Of course, some people consider preserving the environment to be a good thing so they can have pretty places in which to ride their mountain bike. Or go hiking, and try not to get run over by the mountain bikers. Others would say that it's a bit more than that. They would say that the environment—the interconnected network of earth's ecosystems—is the foundation of life. They would point out that it generates the oxygen we breathe, purifies the water we drink, and generates the soil which provides the food we eat. As for our efforts to preserve the environment, they would suggest that calling it an *environmental movement* was a fundamental error. They might suggest that perhaps it should have been called a *sustaining life on earth movement.*

Of course, there are people who think that this is nothing but poppycock, balderdash, and ballyhoo. Some people dismiss the notion that "defying nature defies us" with a look of disapproval and a sweeping hand gesture as if shooing away mosquitos.

If you're one of those people, consider that we choose industrial processes to manufacture our goods, to generate our energy, and to grow our food. And as a direct result, when we go for a drink of nice refreshing water (which goes great with whiskey) it includes organophosphate insecticides, organo-chlorines, dinitro-ortho-cresol, the organophosphate chemicals propetamphos, parathion, disulfoton, thiometon, etrimphos and fenitrothion, as well as metoxuron, benzene, barium, cadmium, and thallium, and also benzelhydrinate, chloriximalia, ardina-tilhyriphorax, and other chemicals with names that are even longer.

I just checked, and these chemicals are *not* on the list of vitamins and minerals necessary to build strong bodies and minds. They are, however, on the list of chemicals that cause cancer, birth defects, and the need to have a laugh track on television shows to know where the funny parts are.

In fact, deaths in the United States from air pollution alone (not counting other forms of pollution, such as the comment strings on online news articles) is conservatively estimated at over 130,000 per year. This should be cause for great concern. If you happen to be one of those 130,000, never mind because you're dead.

There's this COVID-19 thing you might have heard of. It was caused by defying nature. It was the latest in a long line of deadly epidemics, such as Ebola, SARS, and AIDS, which were caused by the disruption of ecosystems and the destruction of biodiversity. This resulted in conditions in which viruses could arise and be more easily transmitted. As one article put it, "Humanity has squeezed the world's wildlife in a crushing grip—and viruses have come bursting out."

So maybe this crazy idea of "defying nature defies us" has something to it. Especially since it has caused the collapse of civilizations such as Chaco Canyon.

HAVE YOU EVER BEEN
TO CHACO CANYON?

Chaco Canyon is one of the civilizations profiled in *Collapse*. The civilization was located in what is now the state of New Mexico, whose motto is: "The land where Georgia O'Keeffe painted those cool pictures of floating skulls and flowers that look like vaginas." The ruins of this civilization, which experienced its height between the years 900 and 1150, include the densest concentration of pueblos in the American Southwest.

Those ruins are carefully preserved as Chaco Canyon National Historic Park, where visitors from a collapsing civilization can visit a civilization that's already collapsed. Those visitors could learn valuable lessons regarding collapsing civilizations—if they felt like it—instead of complaining about the heat and hoping that the nearest burger place has decent milkshakes.

Visitors to the park, when not thinking about milkshakes, are surprised at how the arid and barren landscape could have supported a major civilization. If they had bothered to read the interpretive materials at the visitor center, they would have learned that the region was once far more hospitable, and that the barren landscape is partially a result of the choices made by that civilization.

The region was once forested, but the trees were cut down for timber and firewood. This resulted in a decline in water tables. Unsustainable agricultural practices resulted in lost soil fertility. After depleting local resources, the civilization extended its influence to deplete resources from outlying areas. The population became divided between a well-fed elite living in relative luxury at the pueblos, and outlying populations of a less well-fed peasantry doing the work.

Sound familiar?

The devastation continued, until the environment could no longer support the population. As a result, social differences became meaningless as the entire civilization collapsed.

This might not sound familiar right now, but give it a little time.

Chaco Canyon collapsed because of specific choices regarding how their civilization interacted with their environment. If visitors to Chaco Canyon would actually read the interpretive materials, they might find it interesting to consider that our civilization is making the identical choices. The only thing I can say is, I hope that after their visit they find a burger place with good milkshakes. Enjoy those milkshakes while you can, folks!

HAVE YOU EVER BEEN
TO EASTER ISLAND?

Let's turn to another civilization profiled in *Collapse*. The case of Easter Island is instructive. You know about Easter Island, right? That's the place where the inhabitants carved those mysterious statues of giant heads out of immense blocks of rock. Then they transported those statues for miles without the use of Ford trucks, such as the F-150 which has the highest load rating of any truck in its class.

Easter Island was once covered with forests. As far as we can tell, logs from the trees were used as giant rollers or rails to transport the immense stone statues all over the island. This was necessary since Ford trucks wouldn't be built for another 800 years. But when they were, they would be *Built Ford Tough*.

From what we can gather, the purpose of those immense stone status was an appeal to the Gods to please invent those trucks, because... Well, have you ever tried pushing immense stone statues all over an island? In addition to an appeal to the Gods to invent trucks, the statues were used by the religious and political leaders to signify their status, and therefore to justify not being the ones pushing those immense stone statues all over the island.

Other things besides Ford trucks had not been invented. Such as the concept of "forest management," including the most rudimentary principle of forest management: To manage a forest you must have a forest to manage.

Rather than going through the trouble of inventing the concept of forest management, they eliminated the forests. The result was loss of soil fertility as well as massive soil erosion. Wildlife vanished. Crops failed. Freshwater disappeared. The population engaged in warfare over the last meager resources. Nobody was able to escape the island, since there were no more trees that could be used to construct boats.

Oops!

The final battle between the last two survivors was really pitiful. There was no metal to make knives or other decent weapons. Since the trees were long gone, they couldn't even have a fight with pointed sticks. The final battle was along a beach, where the last two survivors slapped each other with pieces of seaweed in a fight over which one was more pathetic. The result? It was a tie.

WHAT ABOUT OTHER CIVILIZATIONS?

Even in cases where environmental destruction wasn't the primary cause, it was an important secondary cause. Such as with the collapse of Rome. Your grade school teacher Ms. Olifson told you the collapse was due to being defeated by invading hordes of stinky guys with heavy beards and bad breath. Yes, but Rome was weakened and thus able to be defeated because of environmental destruction. Also, by too many orgies. You didn't learn this in school because Ms. Olifson wasn't aware of the environmental destruction and wasn't allowed to tell you about the orgies.

EASTER ISLAND AS MICROCOSM

Most of the civilizations profiled in *Collapse* had complex relationships with other civilizations that effected their decline and fall. The case of Easter Island, however, provides us with a somewhat "pure" example. The remote civilization was totally self-contained, therefore we can think of Easter Island as a microcosm of all earthly civilization.

The civilization of Easter Island was made up of various tribes or clans that sometimes clashed yet were also dependent on each other for trade. And they were all collectively dependent on the resources of their small island.

Consider that all earthly civilization is made up of various nation-states that sometimes clash yet are also dependent on each other for trade. And we're all collectively dependent on the resources of our small planet.

Therefore, Easter Island is a perfect demonstration of where we're headed if we continue in the same direction. And we're continuing in the same direction.

POLITICAL RAMIFICATIONS
OF EASTER ISLAND

Easter Island's elites justified their status by claiming a special relationship to the Gods that would bring prosperity and bountiful harvests. When those harvests ended, the privileged status of the elites could no longer be justified and the statues were toppled. As the religion of the elites was rejected, so were the symbols of that religion.

Comparisons with America are impossible to avoid. In the case of America, we place our greatest faith in the "secular religion" of economic growth. As with Easter Island, American elites justify their power on the basis of their special relationship with the "priests" of the economic system—the bankers, financiers, investors, and business leaders who speak the esoteric language of economics. These priests claim that the power of economic growth is beyond full human understanding, and sacrificing to that power will bring prosperity and bountiful harvests.

As with Easter Island, we can look forward to the time when our secular religion will not be able to save us, and the privileged status of the elites will no longer be justified. Sacrificing for the economy will no longer bring prosperity and bountiful harvests, but some things can be sacrificed to make us feel better. Just imagine the expressions on the faces of those elites when they encounter the return of the guillotine.

A REBUTTAL FROM THAT RANDOM GUY, AND THIS AUTHOR'S WELL-REASONED REPLY

Of course, many people consider that—

Hey, what do we have here? It's that random guy again, running up to me while chewing on a teriyaki stick.

Hey, you're back!

"Yes. I returned in order to advance a proposition that questions your conclusions."

By all means! We're on a journey together toward truth, and our voices reflect different perspectives that can work together synergistically to arrive at more accurate conclusions.

"That's great. I thought maybe you were going to yell at me and take my teriyaki stick."

Of course not! What's the proposition you wish to advance?

"Okay, here goes: A case like Easter Island doesn't apply to us, since they were a primitive society and we're advanced. For example, we have amazingly complex technology that allows us to watch sitcoms and game shows in the comfort of our homes."

That's a very interesting proposition, and one that I imagine is shared by many people. I'll reply to your proposition below, by writing in my book. You can read it later. I'll sell you a free copy for only twenty dollars.

"Wow, that's quite a... Hey, wait a minute!"

So, here's my reply... Yes, we're technologically advanced, but the question—concerning environmental destruction—is whether that's good or bad. The Easter Islanders were basically a stone-age civilization. As a result, it took them centuries to entirely deforest their island.

As for us, we have giant earthmoving equipment and machines that can level a forest in a matter of days. As a result, our rate of deforestation is thousands of times faster. It took the Easter Islanders centuries to lose their topsoil. As for us, consider that in Iowa—one of this country's most productive agricultural states—there are areas that have lost half of their topsoil in only 150 years.

Yay for our technologically advanced civilization!

But it can be argued that the more important thing is that we're *intellectually* advanced. For example, the Easter Islanders were totally ignorant of ecological realities. They had no idea what they were doing. As for us, we know *exactly* what we're doing. Whereas the Easter Islanders were destroying themselves out of ignorance, we're destroying ourselves because we're stupid.

Yay for our intellectually advanced civilization!

By the way, teriyaki sticks provide quality high-protein nutrition with no carbohydrates. If you enjoy teriyaki sticks, I highly recommend teriyaki sticks made by Tillamook Country Smoker, handcrafted with real hardwood smoke on the Oregon coast.

NO SHORTAGE OF SHORTAGES

We're facing shortages of nearly everything. Perhaps most critically, for those of us who drink water, we're rapidly running out of water. The Ogallala Aquifer—the source of 30 percent of America's groundwater used for agricultural irrigation—is nearly empty. So are many other aquifers. Many Western States depend on the Colorado River, which is no longer able to keep up with the demand. Nevada is drilling an immense "drainpipe" under Lake Mead so when the situation gets desperate the state can capture the entire flow of the Colorado River for itself. Of course, downstream regions that also depend on the river will be angry, but they won't be able to yell very loud as a result of dying of thirst.

What about Phoenix? In addition to draining its aquifers, Phoenix has continued to water its 200 golf courses by sucking water out of the Colorado River. What will happen if the river runs dry? Would Phoenix have to stop sucking? No, of course not! Any day now, watch for the governor of Arizona to propose building a 2,000-mile pipeline to Duluth, Minnesota, so Arizona can suck the water out of Lake Superior. Since Lake Superior contains ten percent of all fresh water on earth, Phoenix can continue to suck for a long time.

SELF-EXTINCTION BY RUNNING OUT OF OIL?

This fun-loving author once considered peak oil to be number one on the list of potential causes of our imminent self-destruction. But now this author isn't quite so sure. But let's explore the issue "just for fun" like two friends discussing what part of the chicken that "chicken nuggets" come from.

Question: What is the source of essentially all energy on earth?
Answer: The sun.

It's true! Fossil fuels (such as oil and coal) are the result of millions (or is it billions?) of years of stored solar energy. Which means they're finite.

It's not a serious problem at the moment, but it's important for us to consider. Because our manufacturing, transportation, energy, agriculture, and economy are absolutely dependent on fossil fuels in general, but most of all on oil. And oil is running out.

HOW MUCH OIL IS LEFT?

Nobody is really sure. Maybe oil won't run out for us or our children? Maybe it will be our grandchildren who are stuck up the proverbial tree without a paddle?

Wait... That makes no sense.

The question is complicated. Not the question of *whether* we'll run out of oil, but *when*. Part of the problem is that the people telling us there's a lot of oil left are—to put it as delicately as possible—a bunch of lying jerks. As the font of all knowledge (Wikipedia) put it:

> One difficulty in forecasting the date of peak oil is the opacity surrounding the oil reserves classified as "proven." For the most part, proven reserves are stated by the oil companies, the producer states, and the consumer states. All three have reasons to overstate their proven reserves.

Some oil industry folks are actually admitting that oil is running out! Amazing! But strangely, they're declaring that this isn't a problem. John Hofmeister, the president of Royal Dutch Shell's U.S. operations, says: Don't worry, we can tap other sources of oil, such as the tar sands of Canada, and oil shale in Colorado, Utah, and Wyoming. Clive Mather, CEO of Shell Canada, said the Earth's supply of bitumen hydrocarbons is "almost infinite." (This author needs to do research into what "almost infinite" means. I thought our two choices were *finite* or *infinite*. I didn't realize there were "in-between" choices.) Attorney and mechanical engineer Peter W. Huber, author of *Hard Green: Saving the Environment from the Environmentalists*, claims that "The tar sands of Alberta alone contain enough hydrocarbon to fuel the entire planet for over 100 years."

So I guess we're okay for the next 100 years? Assuming that all of these folks are telling the truth. And assuming that we're willing to live with the effects of scraping those last hydrocarbons off the earth's surface. If you want to spend an evening not having fun, do some research into what's involved in getting the hydrocarbons out of oil shale and tar sands. Make sure you're already depressed, so you don't spoil a good mood.

WHAT WOULD BE THE EFFECTS OF BURNING FOSSIL FUELS FOR THE NEXT HUNDRED YEARS?

Great question! The answer is one of those "bad news, good news" things. Continuing to burn fossil fuels will push us past several "tipping points" that will result in an uncontrollable climate crisis and the destruction of human civilization by way of global warming. But on the other hand, we can enjoy road trips until then.

BUT WON'T ELECTRIC CARS AND ALTERNATIVE ENERGY SAVE US?

Hahaha! I'll get to you later.

SCIENTISTS ARE WORRIED

Scientists, who are much smarter than you, are sounding an extremely urgent alarm. Keep in mind that scientists, by disposition and/or training (or as a scientist might put it, by nature and/or nurture) are clear-headed, sensible, rational, understated people. They're the kind of people who, in describing that their head is on fire, might say, "There appears to be an oxidation phenomenon occurring in my cranial region." They're not prone to hyperbole or exaggeration, unless they've been drinking gin.

This brings us to how the scientists phrase their extremely urgent alarms about the state of the world. They like to use the phrase "dire situation" in describing the effects of destroying our life-support system. In regular-person talk (or drunk-scientist talk) "dire situation" translates to, "We're DOOOOMED!"

Several news articles made kind of a big deal about a report published by the Intergovernmental Science-Policy Platform on Biodiversity and Ecosystem Services (IPBES). According to the report, 1,000,000 species are threatened with extinction as a result of activity by one species (us). According to Sir Robert Watson, one of the scientists that produced the report:

> The overwhelming evidence of the IPBES Global Assessment, from a wide range of different fields of knowledge, presents an ominous picture. The health of ecosystems on which we and all other species depend is deteriorating more rapidly than ever. We are eroding the very foundations of our economies, livelihoods, food security, health, and quality of life worldwide.

I don't know about you, but I'd say that Sir Robert Watson is in danger of being perceived as a "Grumpy Gus"!

This author could do extensive research in order to list a bunch of boring statistics about the rate of deforestation, fishery depletion, coral reef die-offs, loss of soil fertility, etc., etc., etc. But boring statistics are boring. Don't you wish that some smart "scientific types" would add it all together and give us the executive summary of how the earth is doing? Well, the good news is they've already done it! Here's an excerpt from a recent article:

> A team of scientists combined all of humanity's uses of the earth's natural assets into a single indicator—the ecological footprint. The authors concluded that humanity's collective demands first surpassed the earth's regenerative capacity in 1980. By 2000, the demands on the earth's natural systems exceeded sustainable yields by 20 percent. The latest calculations show the excess demand at 50 percent.
>
> In other words, we are no longer living off nature's "interest" but are now consuming the "capital" on which all life depends. Soon, earth's "capital" will be used up and a mass die-off of earthly life will inevitably follow.

Just as a reminder, humanity is a form of earthly life.

I'm proud to say that America has the biggest ecological footprint in the world. Yay for America! We're number one! If you're an American guy you might think this is great news, because you've heard that women prefer men with big footprints. Sorry to disappoint you, but you're thinking of a different kind of footprint.

THE GOVERNMENT IS WORRIED, BUT FOR DIFFERENT REASONS THAN THE REST OF US

There's this thing called "global warming" or "climate change," which this author referred to previously. I'm sure you've heard about it—and are sick of hearing about it. So I won't waste your time explaining things that you already know.

You're welcome!

But a lot of people don't believe that the whole "climate change" thing is real—or that it's serious. Apparently they believe it's a conspiracy by wacko conspiracy theory people. Well, some of the wacko conspiracy theory people who believe it are folks who work in the Pentagon. Yes—that crazy five-sided building full of generals getting lost. Whose idea was it to build a five-sided building, anyway?

Do we need to mention that people working in the Pentagon are smarter than you? Sure they get lost in there, but you would get *more* lost.

The Department of Defense has released several reports expressing its belief that climate change will result in an unprecedented increase in flooding, drought, wildfires, and desertification. Oh no, that will be bad for people!

It will be especially bad—conclude the reports created by military people—for military people. The military isn't concerned about doing something about the climate threats, such as stopping them. It's concerned about the people at military bases who will be put in the non-fun position of dealing with it. According to the Department of Defense Army Modernization Strategy, the government would need to deal with a resurgence of "anti-government and radical ideologies that potentially threaten government stability."

Really? The government thinks that the American people—led into a disaster by a government that did nothing to prevent it—might have bad feelings about the government? Although none of the reports mention it, perhaps the people who wrote the reports were thinking about guillotines?

If you work at the government, there's no need to worry. There's no need to lose your head over the prospect of losing your head. Because if YouTube videos such as *How to Build a Guillotine for Two Hundred Dollars* get too many views, the government has a plan.

Perhaps you're lucky enough to have read the delightful Department of Defense Directive 3025.18, "Defense Support of Civil Authorities"? It outlines the conditions under which federal military forces could be used to put down civil unrest. It tries to sound reassuring, with such words as this:

> Federal military forces shall not be used to quell civil disturbances unless specifically authorized by the president in accordance with applicable law or permitted under emergency authority.

That's not super-reassuring. Why do I suspect that the president, if angry crowds were storming the White House, might be in an authorizing mood?

But wait... What if the president can't be found? What if the president is in a bunker or is in Air Force One on the way to a fortified compound in New Zealand? Don't worry, government people, because The Department of Defense has your back. Because Directive 3025.18 provides carte blanche temporary authority to federal commanders when the president is hiding or running away:

> In these circumstances, those federal military commanders have the authority, in extraordinary emergency circumstances where prior authorization by the president is impossible and duly constituted local authorities are unable to control the situation,

to engage temporarily in activities that are necessary to quell large-scale, unexpected civil disturbances.

Perhaps you were wondering: Can the Department of Defense use drones against American citizens? According to the appropriations bill that authorized the directive:

> The Army shall retain responsibility for and operational control of the MQ-1C Gray Eagle Unmanned Aerial Vehicle (UAV) in order to support the Secretary of Defense.

And in case you were wondering, the MQ-1C Gray Eagle Unmanned Aerial Vehicle is capable of being fully weaponized.

So, don't worry, American citizens! The government acknowledges that social collapse is immanent, and is preparing to deal with it by defending itself against you.

BILLIONAIRES ARE WORRIED, BUT FOR DIFFERENT REASONS THAN US NON-BILLIONAIRES

Perhaps you don't see any reason to worry about the collapse of our civilization. Perhaps you find the whole idea preposterous, even if you don't know what the word *preposterous* means. A lot of billionaires don't think the notion is preposterous, and they *definitely* know what the word means. That's because they're smarter than the rest of us. *That's one reason why they're billionaires.*

Whether or not you're worried about the inevitable collapse of our civilization, they're worried about it. Of course, their worry is somewhat alleviated by the fact that all their dollars (billions of them) gives them the means to purchase escape properties with fortified bunkers.

Talk about using money to insulate yourself from society's problems!

But their worry isn't *totally* alleviated. Their money has provided them a place to go when civilization collapses. And it has given them the means to live without money—which is important, since the big numbers in their bank accounts won't mean too much when there are no more banks. But the lack of money has one major shortcoming that has the billionaires deeply worried.

Their concern was expressed in an article entitled "Survival of the Richest" by Douglas Rushkoff. It's about what happened when Rushkoff—respected as a very smart dude with valuable insights about the future—was invited to meet with a small audience of billionaires from the hedge fund world.

Most of their questions were about how they could defend those escape properties after the collapse. Because they would need security forces to protect them from throngs of hungry people pointing to their property and saying, "Hey, that rich guy in the compound probably has lots of chips and salsa."

Here's where the lack of money becomes a major problem: Without money, how do you retain and control those security forces? Perhaps the security forces could be controlled with disciplinary collars? Perhaps they could be controlled by securing the food supply behind locks that only the billionaires could open?

Rushkoff made the bold suggestion that, rather than control the security forces with discipline and fear, treat them well and make them partners in the operation.

Absurd!

It was at this point that the respect the billionaires held for Rushkoff...

Hey, where'd it go? It was here a minute ago.

So the billionaires abandoned Rushkoff, and went off in search for another very smart dude that could tell them about security forces that could be radio-controlled by devices implanted in their brains.

Which brings us to consider a very interesting question: Are billionaires selfish? Or is it that they only care about themselves?

WHAT JARED DIAMOND THINKS OF
OUR CHANCES OF AVOIDING COLLAPSE

In the concluding chapter of *Collapse*, Jared Diamond reports that he's a "cautious optimist." Your devoted author, when reading this, was somewhat confused. Because everything he'd written up to that point demonstrated (clearly and with tons of evidence) that we're on a path leading to collapse if we don't change. But if that's the case, then how can he have any optimism at all?

Because, he reasons, we could change if we wanted to.

But consider, gentle reader, the possibility that we don't want to change. In that case, I believe that rather than "cautious optimism" the appropriate response should be "stock the compound with non-perishables and prepare to defend the perimeter."

Because the change would need to be somewhat more than "recycle our coffee cozies." The change would need be more like "recycle the assumptions underlying our idea of civilization." And we don't even want to recycle our coffee cozies.

But a few years later, as your devoted author was writing this chapter, he was pleased to come across an interview with none other than Jared Diamond. The interview was about his latest book, *Upheaval.* Apparently Mr. Diamond had become a bit less of a "cautious optimist." In the course of the interview, when asked about the likelihood of total social collapse, he answered, "I would estimate the chances are about 49 percent that the world as we know it will collapse by about 2050."

That was very interesting to this author, who had imagined that collapse would occur soon after 2050. Also, this author had recently come across a news item (via CBS News) about the results of a study by an international team of ecologists and economists. The news item—concerning the extinction of salt-water fish—was entitled, "The apocalypse has a new date: 2048." So this fun-loving author is predicting collapse at roughly the same time as the respected and very-intelligent Jared Diamond and an international team of ecologists and economists.

I would be tempted to consider this as an example of "great minds think alike," except that this fun-loving author doesn't have a great mind. This fun-loving author isn't exceptionally smart, and only thinks as a part-time hobby. Who wants to be a professional full-time thinker? That doesn't sound fun at all.

WHAT KIND OF WINE GOES WITH HUMAN?

One of the most interesting things in *Collapse* is a fascinating tidbit about the last survivors of a collapsing civilization.

Question: When the food supply runs out, what do people eat?
Answer: Each other.

It's true! Every collapsing culture known to history has resorted to cannibalism. There's substantial archeological evidence that, in the late stages of social collapse, people cooked and ate other people. However, to the best of this author's knowledge, there are no surviving records of the recipes.

AND NOW, LET'S EXPLORE THE
REASONS *WHY* WE'RE DOOMED

Earlier, in the introduction to this lovely book, I mentioned that I would ease your troubled mind by convincing you that you're not crazy in thinking that we're doomed. And that I would make you feel less crazy by helping you understand *why* we're doomed. So now, without further ado, let's move on to the critically important question, to be explored thoroughly and with all the seriousness it deserves: *Why is we doomed?*

CHAPTER 3

THE LOVE OF MONEY IS WHAT KEEPS THE ECONOMY FROM COLLAPSING

In our civilization, economic considerations overshadow all other considerations. And of all the economic considerations, one can't help but notice the emphasis on economic growth. Media reports focus almost exclusively on whether the economy is growing, or on whether it's growing fast enough. One is struck at how this indicator is given such importance and other indicators are ignored, such as whether people are living in boxes and getting their meals from dumpsters. It also might be nice if other indicators were included, such as whether the capacity of the planet to sustain life is being destroyed.

Our economic indicators are distorted. I'm not the first person to have noticed that as the official economic indicators have risen, our society has been rapidly degrading. As I'm writing these words, the official economic indicators tell us that the economy is healthy. But this diagnosis can in no way be applied to what's going on in the country. Among the industrialized nations, America has the highest poverty rate, the lowest score on the United Nations index of material well-being of children, the highest health care expenditures, the highest infant mortality rate, the highest prevalence of mental health problems, the highest obesity rate, the highest consumption of antidepressants per capita, the highest homicide rate, and the largest prison population per capita.

When a decision needs to be made, we seldom (never) hear anybody say, "We should make the decision based on what's the right thing to do, on what's good and wise, on what's best for people and for the long-term good of society." We generally (always) hear, "We should make the decision based on what will enhance economic growth."

The assumption seems to be that more economic growth *is* what's good and wise, and best for people and the long-term good of society. This is the assumption of quite a few economists, who claim that it does this automatically via what they call the "invisible hand."

But the correlation doesn't seem to be correlating. The economy continues to grow, but the good stuff ain't happening. In fact, as the economy continues goin' up, all the other indicators are goin' down.

The invisible hand seems to be slacking on the job. That is, if it's still around. Maybe it got tired of working for the economy and got a better offer from Hollywood? If it's invisible, how can we tell if it's still here? Maybe if it was visible, we'd see that the invisible hand is giving us the middle finger?

LET'S MOVE ON TO QUESTIONS THAT WE MIGHT ACTUALLY BE ABLE TO ANSWER

Turning our attention to our current economic system, we're led to ask: Does our current economic system affirm life?

If you answered "Yes" I have a great investment opportunity for you. Mail a signed check to this author. No need to fill in the amount, I'll take care of that later. Trust me.

If you answered, "I suspect that our current economic system does *not* affirm life, but I can't put my finger on exactly why and it would sure be great to have it explained in more detail," then you're in the right place at the right time. Obviously you're too savvy to fall for my investment opportunity (scam). But feel free to send some beer money. Or some beer. I'm not picky, although I prefer dark ales. A pale ale would be fine, but please no IPAs. If you have whiskey, that would be fine too. I'm not picky, although I prefer Irish whiskey.

MY QUALIFICATIONS?

Is this author qualified to discuss the relationship of economics to life? Consider all of the economic policies currently in place in the entire world. How many of them are focused on the relationship of economics to life? The answer is: *None*. Also, how many of the people controlling our economic system go roller skating? The answer is: *None*. As a result, nothing about roller skating—how it's a fun and healthy activity for the whole family, how skating rinks should be encouraged—makes any difference in economic policy.

As for the relationship of economics to life, even if you study economics for years—even if you read stacks of thick books on the subject, even if you achieve an advanced degree in economics—*you will not encounter a single discussion of the relationship of economics to life*.

Isn't that kind of... oh, I don't know... *weird?*

So even though I'm not an official economist, I'm the only one in the world that's focused exclusively on the topic. Therefore, *I'm the world's leading expert on the relationship of economics to life*. That's what makes me immanently qualified. Or eminently qualified. One of those.

PROBLEMS? WHAT PROBLEMS?

Could it be that there are some problems with our economic system? There are many good things about it, let's not forget that. Our economic system has greatly enhanced our material standard of living. Across America, nearly all of us can afford a flat-screen high-definition television to watch commercials telling us to buy a Chicken Gordita at Taco Bell.

By the way, did you know that this week Taco Bell is having a special deal on Chicken Gorditas? That's right! Buy two Chicken

Gorditas at the regular price and you can get a third for the price of another one.

But consider that other aspects of our economic system aren't quite so positive. Let's consider some questions we could ask of our economic system.

Why does the economy so often seem to be against things you'd think we want to encourage—such as environmental protection, health care, affordable housing, and social justice? Why is full employment bad for the economy? Why does poverty increase as a minority of us gets increasingly rich, and why do we accept an economic system that concludes the solution is more money for the rich? Why is economic insecurity and stress increasing? Why do we need to run continuously faster just to keep from falling behind? And why is the justification for all of this always: "Sorry, but we can't afford to do otherwise"?

America is the richest county in the history of human civilization. With so much material abundance, we should be in the midst of a kind of "golden age." For perhaps the first time in human history, we could easily provide basic needs to everyone.

But we don't. Our economic system won't let us.

Why is this the case? And even though economic growth isn't solving any of the problems, why is economic growth still considered to be the solution to all the problems?

We can't ask the economic system, since it lacks the ability of speech. We can, however, ask an apologist for the system—a person that has internalized the logic and assumptions of the system. In other words, a person that makes every decision based on maximizing economic return, a person for whom "liquid assets" refers to something other than the contents of their liquor cabinet, a person who—

Oh! Here comes an apologist for the system!

Hello there, apologist for the system! Can we do a brief interview?

"How much am I getting paid?"

Publicity!

"No cash?"

How about if I plug your latest book?

"You've got five minutes."

With us today is Phatt Wallet, the author of MONEY FIXES EVERYTHING, Economic Growth is the Solution to All of Our Problems. Thank you for joining us today, Mr. Wallet.

"You've got four minutes."

First question. How can economic growth fix the problem of poverty?

"If the problem is that people don't have enough money, then the solution is more money."

But instead of more money, maybe the people on the top could share more with people on the bottom.

"What are you, a Communist? Or a Christian?"

But the economy has grown tremendously over the past several decades, and poverty hasn't decreased. In fact, it has increased.

"Which means that we need to grow the economy even faster."

I'm not sure if I follow your—

"Next question. You have three minutes."

What about the problem of unemployment?

"Only with substantial economic growth can companies afford to hire more workers."

How do you explain that even when the economy is thriving there's still substantial unemployment?

"That can be explained by the job-killing taxes imposed by our government."

But companies are getting more and more tax breaks, and even companies that pay essentially no taxes continue layoffs and downsizing."

"Next question."

Housing is becoming increasingly unaffordable. How can economic growth solve this problem?

"Simple. If the economy grows, then people will have more money to afford housing."

What about just making housing more affordable?

"I do not consider it a 'solution' to give people the option of living in rat-infested shacks or mud huts."

Wait a minute, just because a home is affordable doesn't mean—

"Two minutes."

What about the problem of pollution and environmental destruction?

"Cleaning up pollution is very expensive, therefore to afford it we need substantial economic growth. In addition, more environmentally-friendly methods of conducting business are more expensive, therefore to avoid environmental destruction we need more economic growth."

But economic growth is a main driver of pollution and environmental destruction. Are you saying that we have to destroy the earth so we can afford to save it?

"How else can we afford to save it?"

But wait a minute, that's—

"Sorry, that's all the time you get."

Goodbye and thank you for your time, apologist for the system!

I don't know about you, gentle reader, but based on what the apologist for the system related to us, I believe there may be some problems with the assumptions underlying our economic system.

METAPHYSICAL FOUNDATIONS

As some wise person once wrote, "I believe there may be some problems with the assumptions underlying our economic system."

Oh wait—that was *me!* I forgot that I wrote it, and assumed that it was written by the leading expert on the relationship of economics to life.

Oh wait—it *was!*

Well, it looks like it's time to look more deeply into those assumptions. I guess it's time to ask the question: *What's the metaphysical foundation of our economic system?*

You probably weren't expecting that.

But here's a thought to consider: *Everything has a metaphysical foundation.* It's an important thought, in my opinion. And not just because I'm the one who thought it.

Is that right? Am I the one who *thought* it? Or am I the one who *thinked* it? Or *thunk* it? It arrived with a "thunk" so that's probably the right word.

My own thunk agrees with that of the economist and philosopher E.F. Schumacher, who wrote: "No system or machinery or economic doctrine or theory stands on its own feet: it is invariably built on a metaphysical foundation, that is to say, upon our basic outlook on life, its meaning and its purpose."

Since our economic system has a metaphysical foundation, it's probably a good idea to know what it is so we can decide if it's a good metaphysical foundation or a sucky one.

A FUN FACT CONCERNING
THE EXCITING TOPIC OF
METAPHYSICAL FOUNDATIONS

An important aspect of that foundation has to do with the relationship of economics to nature, to the overall system of interconnected life on which we're dependent. Unfortunately, that foundation is not what you would call "positive." According to John Locke, who laid the intellectual foundation for capitalism, "The negation of nature is the way toward happiness." And if you believe that all of our economic problems are the result of capitalism, it might be good to recall that, according to Karl Marx, who laid the intellectual foundation for communism, "Man of his own accord starts, regulates, and controls the material re-actions between himself and nature. He opposes himself to Nature."

Did you assume that capitalism and communism had different metaphysical foundations? Do you know what they say about having assumptions?

The idea that nature should be negated and opposed isn't a good metaphysical foundation regarding the processes of life that we're dependent on. Also, it's not good for the all the other species besides humans that would probably prefer not to be negated and opposed. Believe it or not, some people believe that other species have a right to exist just for the sake of their own existence. Of course, such people contribute nothing to economic growth and can therefore be negated and opposed.

FOR AN ACCURATE COST-BENEFIT
ANALYSIS, YOU NEED TO
ACCURATELY COUNT COSTS

One of our fundamental economic principles is *throughput*: the conversion of physical resources into economic resources. In other words, into money. The more throughput, the more money.

Cut down a tree, find someone to give you a buck for it—presto-chango, you're now a buck richer. Cut down a bazillion trees—hey, a bazillion bucks! What a deal! But the more money we make, the more we destroy the environment.

Oops!

We don't count the costs of that destruction because, according to the metaphysical foundation of our economic system, nature has no value. As Herman Daly, an actual real-life economist who you've never heard of, put it: "We write off the value of man-made assets against current production as they depreciate, but make no such deduction for the depreciation of natural assets. A country could exhaust its mines, cut down its forests, erode its topsoil, and exploit its wildlife and fisheries to extinction, and measured income would rise steadily as these assets disappeared."

Our economic system doesn't count the costs of resource depletion, or the costs of pollution, or the costs of repairing ecological damage. In economic terms, such costs are *externalities*—meaning that they're *external* to economic considerations. Here's a brilliant definition of *externality* formulated by the world's leading expert on the relationship of economics to life: "An externality is a cost of economic activity that is not paid by the individual or organization that profits by the activity."

By market standards, burning fossil fuels is the least expensive form of energy because the economy doesn't recognize the costs of global warming, respiratory disease, and many other environmental and social consequences. In economic terms, it *externalizes* those costs. Similarly, industrial agriculture is the least expensive way to produce food only because it doesn't count the costs of eroded soils, depleted aquifers, pesticide contamination, and nutritionally-poor food.

The free-enterprise market economy is efficient—that's one of its positive features. But it's efficient only in its own context, only in terms of what it counts as important. The ability of the planet to sustain life doesn't enter the cost-benefit analysis. It doesn't figure into the "bottom line." By ignoring life's "bottom line," it seeks the most efficient way to go the most destructive direction.

This could be fixed. I'll explain how that's possible later, as well as why there's not a chance in hell we'll actually do it. But first, there's a deeper problem that there's not a chance in hell we'll fix.

THE GROWTH IMPERATIVE

The main problem is that... *how do I put this gently?...* we not only *like* to destroy the environment for profit, but we *have* to. Unfortunately, we're... *sorry, but this isn't easy...* we're *addicted* to it.

There! I said it! It's out in the open now!

Perhaps you don't believe me. Perhaps you've noticed a distinct lack of comments by economic experts indicating that we're addicted to destroying the ability of the planet to sustain life.

That's understandable. Such comments are avoided, since they would be "bad public relations" for our economic system. Such comments could cause people to lose faith in our economic system, and to lose faith in the economic experts who comment on it. Such comments could cause those economic experts to lose their high-paying positions and be forced to work at Taco Bell making Chicken Gorditas.

Don't forget: This week only, three for the price of two plus one!

They say it, though, just in a different way—a way that allows them to retain their high-paying positions and keep them far away from Chicken Gorditas. Economists sometimes refer to the *growth imperative.* (If you're not familiar with the word *imperative*, it means "must happen or else the zombies will eat our brains.")

A QUICK NOTE ABOUT ZOMBIES

The fear of zombies is the fear of the advanced capabilities of the human mind—the qualities expressed by the cerebral cortex—

becoming overridden by the primitive reptilian brain with its sole focus on physical survival. This is revealed by the fact that the preferred meal of zombies is human brains. A zombie is a metaphor for primitive humanity killing advanced humanity by consuming it. So when I talk about zombies, I'm not talking about humanity being infected by a weird disease that turns them into the walking dead. I'm talking about the most rudimentary and primitive aspects of ourselves coming into prominence as civilization collapses.

THE GROWTH IMPERATIVE, CONTINUED

As for the growth imperative... Here's a real honest-to-God quotation from Edward Heath, who used to be the Prime Minister of Britain (that's a country in Europe famous for inventing the musical group The Beatles): "The alternative to expansion is not an England of quiet market towns linked only by trains puffing slowly and peacefully through green meadows. The alternative is slums, dangerous roads, old factories, cramped schools, and stunted lives."

Everybody knows, of course, that economic stagnation makes the economy sick. If economic growth slows, the result is a *recession*. Economists don't like to say the word *recession* because people tend to panic. The stock market tends to crash. Then the president has to issue statements such as: "Don't worry, there's absolutely no danger of the economy collapsing, but we need to take drastic action to keep the economy from collapsing." And "drastic action" means "do whatever we can to stimulate the economy." This results in politicians competing to introduce the biggest *stimulus package*.

Gentle reader, you're not the only one to have noticed that this is more than vaguely pornographic. But even if it makes you giggle in delight or blush in embarrassment, we have no choice but to do whatever we can to get the economy to feel tingly all over.

Because if we don't fix the recession, it could lead to a word that economists aren't supposed to say out loud. But I'm not an official economist so I can do whatever I want. If we aren't able to fix the recession, it leads to a *depression!*

It's so cool to not be an official economist! I can even say *economic death spiral* which economists aren't even allowed to think about.

By *depression*, I'm referring to an *economic* depression as opposed to an *emotional* depression. But often they go together, since if you lose your job and are living in a box and your dining options have been reduced to a choice between *grilled pigeon* or *boiled rat* then you probably won't be feeling "on top of the world."

So we stimulate the economy so it can feel healthy again. This is important since we all depend on the economy.

But wait... One of the main ways we stimulate the economy is with a quick infusion of money via an increase in throughput. In other words, via an increase in environmental destruction. This is bad since we all depend on the environment.

The economy must continually grow to remain viable. But how can we have infinite growth on a finite planet? Even when the economy is doing well, environmental protection is opposed on the grounds that it will slow down economic growth. It will hurt businesses and kill jobs. But when the economy *isn't* doing well, the opposition gets worse. Sustainability gets at least some consideration during good economic times. But during an economic downturn, sustainability will be thrown out the window, along with whoever dares to mention it.

"Do not fear," the apologist would have said if he was still here. "We now have an *information economy* which is not tied to physical resources. Therefore, economic growth can continue infinitely without destroying the earth."

Oh no you don't! Not so fast! Our so-called "information economy" is dependent on the resource economy to support it. As the information economy has grown, so has overall consumption. All those "information workers" don't live on information. They require food, housing, energy, transportation, and big-screen television sets to watch commercials for Chicken Gorditas. And if the information economy has truly eliminated the need to destroy the environment, then why is environmental protection still opposed on the grounds that it would be bad for the economy?

If the apologist was *still* here, he probably would have brought up the concept of *decoupling*—the idea that economic growth can be separated from the use of physical resources. But attempts at decoupling have only worked to a very limited degree. In the essay "Why We Have to Give Up on Endless Economic Growth" Dominic Boyer concluded that, according to several studies, "There is scant evidence thus far that decoupling economic growth from resource use is both possible and sustainable."

Could it be that the apologist—along with all the other apologists—are desperately grasping at any justification that it's okay to continue our unsustainable consumption?

THE FUTURE DOESN'T LOOK
SO BRIGHT, SO WE DON'T
NEED TO WEAR SHADES

When Adam Smith developed the economic theories at the heart of modern economics, he predicted that economic progress would stop when we reached the natural limits of the environment. But he thought that those limits were so far in the future that it was irrelevant to his theories. Those limits are no longer irrelevant.

Eventually all addictions "bottom out" and that's what will happen to our economy when earth's resources run out—if not before. Which explains why both the environment and the economy are going down... down... down... At some point the economy—unable to keep the growth addiction going—will collapse. Therefore, the endgame of a growth-based economy is a destroyed planet and collapsed economy. It's simply a matter of which goes first.

Somehow it doesn't seem right that we have to choose one or the other. Can't we make things so we can choose both? Can't we have economic prosperity *and* environmental health?

GOOD QUESTION!

The answer, in our current economic system, is: *No we can't.*

WHAT?

We can't? Why not? How in heck did this happen? How did we become addicted to economic growth? Why is it that—

Hold on, an economist is coming this way, and they do *not* look pleased.

"Hey! Don't use that word *addicted.* Because we're not addicted!"

Sorry! Let me try again... How did it happen that if we fail to grow the economy then it will collapse and take down human civilization with it?

"Much better! Please proceed."

Would you care to stick around? Your expertise could be very helpful.

"Sorry, but I must be going. I have a very important meeting with the House Finance Committee to figure out how to enlarge their stimulus package."

Have you tried www.hotnudeteens.com?

"I'm not familiar with that one, but I'll bring it up with the committee. Thank you American Citizen for helping to keep America free of economic collapse."

You're welcome, and good luck!

Okay, now that the economist is gone... Here we go toward answering the very important question: *How did we become addicted to economic growth?*

A SIMPLE QUESTION WITH
AN ANSWER THAT WILL
ROCK YOU TO YOUR CORE

The answer is directly related to the answer to the seldom-asked question: *Where does money come from?* When I began exploring this question many years ago, I was surprised to discover that the answer isn't easy to find. Textbooks of basic economics generally avoid this very basic question.

I asked many people, some of whom weren't alcoholics, and often received the answer: *Money is printed by the government.* Incredibly, this answer is widely believed. But even a non-economist like me realized this couldn't be the answer, since only a tiny percentage of money exists as printed currency.

Although the government doesn't introduce money by printing it, there *is* a sense in which money is introduced by the government. This is the dynamic by which the Federal Reserve loans money to the Treasury, which uses it to pay for government expenses. Thus, additional money enters the American economy.

Although essentially true as far as it goes, this answer is misleading because it neglects to account for a vitally important fact: The dynamic doesn't introduce *money*; it introduces *debt*. The "money" created is in the form of a loan that needs to be paid back. The addition of a trillion dollars to the economy is accompanied by adding a trillion dollars to the national debt. And that debt needs to be paid off somehow. This also applies to other strategies, such as electronic credits and quantitative easing. These strategies result in a short-term boost of money into the economy, but only by creating government debt.

With all of these dynamics, the only way to pay off the debt is by the overall growth of the economy, allowing the government—through taxes—to pay off the debt.

But how does the economy grow? Once again, we're back to the question of: *Where does money come from?*

THE ANSWER THAT WILL
ROCK YOU TO YOUR CORE

Money is introduced into existence by banks in the form of interest-bearing loans. What almost nobody realizes is that a loan doesn't consist solely of other people's savings or the assets of the bank. A percentage of every loan is the creation of money that had no prior existence.

The dynamic can be traced to seventeenth-century European bankers who figured out a clever way to increase their assets with no additional work. At the time, "money" was a receipt for gold brought to the banker for safekeeping. The bankers realized they could print receipts for which no gold existed. This would work as long as there was enough gold on hand for the small percentage who withdrew it. (This strategy later became what we call the *fractional reserve system.*)

Then they devised another strategy to further increase their assets. By introducing these "receipts" as interest-bearing loans, they could induce others to make money for them in order to pay off the interest.

The dynamic was given governmental blessing in the early eighteenth century, when France saved itself from financial collapse with the establishment of the Banque Royale under John Law. As if by magic, the shuffling of numbers on ledger sheets created money that turned France into a solvent nation. This created the modern concept of a bank as an institution that issues notes in excess of the means to redeem them.

Eventually, the increasing power of banks led to the introduction of all money in the industrialized nations to be made in this way. And after a few hundred years, our current system is only a vastly more complex and sophisticated version of the same dynamic.

Basically, money is an "IOU" issued by a bank. Robert Heilbroner and Lester Thurow (who are actual economic professors) described this in *Economics Explained* (which is an actual book):

> Why is it that banks create money when they make loans, but you and I do not, when we lend money? Because we all accept bank liabilities (deposits) as money, but we do not accept personal or business IOU's to make payments with. You cannot buy groceries with a General Motors IOU, but you can with a Chase Manhattan IOU—a check drawn on your account there.

Money is created by magic, out of nothing but future expectations. But what are the long-term consequences of this "magic"? Or to put it another way, how long can we get something out of nothing? Those loans need to be paid back. Which requires money. But the only way to create more money is with more loans. But then *those* loans need to be paid back with more money. Which requires *more* loans.

Do you see the problem here?

Money needs growth, and growth needs money, and money needs growth. It's a trap, a vicious cycle. In other words... *drum roll, please...* an *addiction*.

Perhaps, gentle reader, it occurred to you that this dynamic is essentially a "pyramid scheme" or "Ponzi scheme"—the fraudulent investment scheme in which an increasing debt is passed on to future investors. And you're aware, of course, that such schemes are doomed to fail. And because of this, such schemes are strictly against the law. But—*oh no!*—our entire economy is based on such a scheme.

It sounds unbelievable—maybe even crazy. But as noted in the introduction to this fascinating book, American physicist and Nobel laureate Steven Chu knows the truth. Yuval Noah Harari, author of the best-selling book *Sapiens, A Brief History of*

Humankind, knows the truth. In that book, after examining the basis of our economic system, he wrote: "It sounds like a giant Ponzi scheme, doesn't it?" He then goes on to confirm that it sounds like a giant Ponzi scheme because it is.

Many people know the truth. Stephanie, one of the bartenders at Darwin's Theory, knows that our economy is based on a pyramid scheme. And she'll be glad to tell you about it, right after she yells at Pirate John to stop singing sea shanties.

EVERYONE IS ALLOWED TO TELL THE TRUTH EXCEPT FOR ECONOMISTS

This is something of an "elephant in the room" for economists. Since acknowledging the elephant would impel them to consider implications that nobody wants to consider, their attitude toward the elephant is: "What elephant?" As a result, the dynamic is unnamed. Which is unfortunate, because such an important dynamic should be named, don't you think?

I'm going to help out the economists here, because we really need a term for this—a *fun* term—for how the more money we have the more we owe.

It's like money goes into a kind of "void." Should we call it *The Money Void*? No, that sounds too passive. The void is alive. It's hungry. It's insatiable. The more you feed it, the hungrier it gets. It's an *addict*. It's got teeth. And claws. And bad breath. I'm going to call it *The Money Pit Junkie Monster*. No matter how much money we feed to The Money Pit Junkie Monster, it will always growl, "Me still hungry! Me want more money! *Grrr!*"

This is much more descriptive than anything an official economist would have come up with. Once again, it's cool—and much more fun—to not be an official economist.

ECONOMICS IN A HISTORICAL VEIN

Here's something interesting. It was written in 1933 by economist John Maynard Keynes. He recognized that it was important to have economic growth. But he felt that it was important that economic growth reach a point where it could stop:

> Suppose that a hundred years hence we are eight times better off than today. The economic problem may be solved. The economic problem is not the permanent problem of the human race.
>
> The economic problem, the struggle for subsistence, always has been the primary, most pressing problem of the human race. Thus for the first time since his creation man will be faced with his real, his permanent problem—how to use his freedom from pressing economic cares, how to live wisely and agreeably and well.
>
> When the accumulation of wealth is no longer of high social importance, there will be great changes in the code of morals. The love of money will be recognized for what it is, a somewhat disgusting morbidity, one of those semi-criminal, semi-pathological propensities which one hands over with a shudder to the specialists in mental disease.
>
> I see us free, therefore, to return to some of the most sure and certain principles of religion and traditional virtue—that avarice is a vice, that the exaction of usury is a misdemeanor, and the love of money is detestable.

That last paragraph introduces some important terms whose meaning might not be clear. *Avarice* means "greed." *Usury* means "charging interest on loans." These are both religious terms. The world's major religions oppose *avarice* as unethical. Technically speaking, the world's major religions also oppose *usury*, although they don't seem to bring it up too much these days. Remember these terms, because they'll come up again.

WHAT DID KEYNES MEAN BY "SEMI-PATHOLOGICAL PROPENSITIES"?

He probably would have used the term *addiction*, but in 1933 the term was used only for alcoholics, drug addicts, and women who love too much.

WHY CAN'T WE LIVE WISELY
AND AGREEBLY AND WELL?

The main problem with the idea of stopping economic growth is that we can't. The introduction of money as interest-bearing debt explains not only how the economy grows, but why it *has* to grow. Unfortunately, we can never get to a point where growth is "enough." We can never achieve the freedom to focus our attention on "how to live wisely and agreeably and well," even if we wanted to.

This is why even though America has more money than any country in history, it still needs more. This is why even as it's becoming increasingly obvious that economic growth isn't solving unemployment or ending poverty or doing any of the other things it's supposedly capable of doing, we keep trying it anyway.

Doing the same thing over and over while expecting a different outcome. That's a definition of *addiction*. It's also a definition of *insanity*.

Is this author suggesting that we're addicted *and* insane?

While you consider that question, let's move on to the next chapter, which explores how our possibly-insane economic system creates, enforces, and exacerbates a variety of serious problems that are effecting you right now in your actual life. For example, how even though you live in the richest country in the history of human civilization, every day you're getting closer to living in a box and getting your meals from dumpsters.

CHAPTER 4

RELATABLE REAL-LIFE EFFECTS OF OUR ADDICTION TO ECONOMIC GROWTH

Money enters the economy through the dynamic of investment and growth, primarily via businesses and corporations. As a result, these institutions receive a disproportionate amount of attention. If we're dependent on economic growth as an overall dynamic, then the tangible focus of that dependence is placed upon the individuals and organizations at the heart of that dynamic.

The heroes of society become the entrepreneurs and business leaders who create growth. Corporate profit becomes synonymous with the economic growth from which we'll all supposedly benefit—or in any case is necessary to keep the economy from collapsing. As a result of this dependence, governments have little choice but to give tax breaks and favors to corporate interests. If state governments ask too much of the wealthy, they'll leave the state. If the federal government asks too much, they'll leave the country. As a result, our democracy is increasingly becoming a business-dominated plutocracy.

Our legal system has evolved to reflect this dependence. Corporations have been legally classified as "persons" that are free to spend billions influencing government with money that's classified as "speech." How's that for bias?

A lot of people are declaring such developments to be results of *late-stage capitalism*. To me, it makes more sense to think of them as results of *late-stage economic growth addiction*.

The addiction to economic growth gives politicians a handy justification for all of this. Whenever a politician is questioned about why they're working to turn the country into a business-dominated plutocracy, all they have to do is to say, "Sorry, I'd love to vote for what's best for the general public and the future of life on earth, but if I don't vote for corporate profit at the expense of everything else, then the economy will collapse and the zombies will eat our brains." It's a much better justification than saying, "I bend over for corporate interests because they fund my ability to hold public office." That justification probably wouldn't be too helpful at re-election time.

A FEW WORDS ABOUT
TRICKLE-DOWN THEORY

Those words are: *It doesn't work*. The idea, of which you are most surely aware, is that we can best help the people "on the bottom" by giving more money to those "on the top." This will spur business investment, resulting in economic growth that will "trickle down" to the people living in boxes. But perhaps you've noticed that we've been giving more to the people on top, but somehow America's "living in a box" population has been increasing.

Supporters of capitalism, from the beginning, have justified the profit motive with the idea that the "invisible hand" will distribute the profits throughout society. This is based on the idea that profits will be reinvested in further production. But because we're addicted to economic growth, we're required to overlook how the tax breaks and financial favors given to the wealthy are often spent in ways that have nothing to do with productive investment. Such as how the profits are used to increase executive salaries to absurd levels. Such as how the profits are diverted to offshore tax havens. Such as how the profits are invested in speculative ventures that extract wealth from the economy without adding anything of value. Such as how the profits are used to purchase escape properties for when America's box-dwelling population becomes an angry mob marching toward them with guillotines.

Yet trickle-down theory can't be abandoned, no matter how many studies show that it doesn't work. Taking action on the results of those studies would oppose too many powerful interests. It would also require acknowledging an elephant in the room that nobody wants to see.

BUYING GROWTH WITH DEBT

In the months following the outbreak of the COVID-19 pandemic, the American economy did something unprecedented. In the April-June quarter of 2020, the economy shrank 33 percent—the worst quarterly plunge in American history. For an economy that must grow or collapse, this was something of a problem.

To keep our economy from collapsing, the Federal Reserve rapidly upped its lending to the government, increasing it by a third to $5.2 trillion—23 percent of gross domestic product. Then the government spent that money on a variety of programs to assist or bail out individuals, businesses, and banks.

Essentially, the government created fake growth. It bought growth with debt. It made up for the lack of real economic growth by creating debt to be paid off in the future.

How? By future growth, of course. Or if that doesn't work, then by increasing taxes. *But wait...* We can't increase taxes too much, because it would reduce consumer spending and further hinder economic growth.

Well, we can just create more fake growth by going further into debt, right? To be paid for by...? Well, not by me. Since I became retired, I don't need to pay taxes.

GLOBAL REAL-LIFE EFFECTS

As a result of the increasing globalization of the economy, everybody on earth has become a de-facto employee of a global financial system that functions as a single world corporation. This has had the effect of putting everyone on earth into a competitive "race to the bottom." This has been working out great for everybody on earth that's in a position to profit by it. As for the other 97 percent of us, it's been working out less great.

In this corporation, as in all corporations, employee wages are considered to be nothing more than an expense to be reduced or eliminated. Outsourcing us is acceptable if it's profitable to those doing the outsourcing. On a related note, replacing us with robots or artificial intelligence is acceptable if it's profitable to those doing the replacing. On another related note, subjecting the remaining employees to increasing pressure and a steady erosion of benefits is acceptable if it's profitable to those applying the pressure and doing the eroding.

All of these developments could be attributed to good old-fashioned greed on the part of national and multinational corporations. But they're always justified and supported by the government as necessary for economic growth. And because we're addicted to economic growth, the government is required to overlook how all of these dynamics result in enormous profits for a small minority, while the rest of us are required to sacrifice. Essentially, we're being asked to sacrifice for the sake of an economy that's trying to get rid of us.

UNEMPLOYMENT SUCKS

A little-known fact of growth-based economics is that it actually *depends* on a certain amount of unemployment. In 1958, an economist by the name of William Phillips noticed that when unemployment rose, wages fell. He summarized his findings in something called the *Phillips Curve*, which charts a relationship based on the dynamic of supply and demand. Picture a teeter-totter with employers on one side, and employees on the other side. A surplus of employees means *low* demand, which forces the employees to compete by accepting *lower* wages. *The employers are winning!* But a *shortage* of employees means *high* demand, which forces the employers to compete by offering *higher* wages. *The employees are winning!*

But if employers have to pay too much in wages, the companies won't be able to expand and they'll stop taking out loans. Economic growth will stop and the economy will collapse. *Everybody loses!* So what does this mean? It means that an economic system addicted to growth—*like ours!*—actually *depends* on a certain amount of unemployment.

Shocking news? Not to businesspeople, who read about it in the business sections of the mainstream media where it's openly discussed. Several years ago, Federal Reserve Board Chairman Alan Greenspan had an *Oops!* moment and publicly expressed concern over what he called "dangerously low levels of unemployment." (Careful Al, you don't want to be quite so *honest* when the microphones are turned on.)

Yet the apologists for our economic system keep telling us that the solution to unemployment is economic growth, even though the conditions that make economic growth possible make unemployment necessary.

Why doesn't anybody tell us this stuff?

Very occasionally, some politician will talk about the goal of full employment. Since this would destroy our economy, we're led to ask an interesting question: Are such politicians totally ignorant of economic reality, or are they shamelessly manipulating us with ideas they know can never be implemented? Are they stupid, or are they just jerking our chains?

Humanity is the only species on earth that requires a portion of the population to be useless. Can you imagine any other species—wolverines, for example—with the policy that five percent of all wolverines are required to lay around and get depressed and drink fortified wine?

THE GOVERNMENT IS LYING TO US ABOUT THE UNEMPLOYMENT RATE

You weren't aware that the government lies to us? Meet me later so I can talk to you about some investment opportunities. I'd like to offer you some very inexpensive oceanfront properties that aren't at all endangered by rising sea levels due to global warming. But for now, it's important to realize that the government isn't quite being honest about the unemployment rate.

If the official unemployment rate often seems suspiciously low, that's because the government does what's called "creative accounting" (lying) in how it determines the rate. It only counts people that have been actively looking for work within the past four weeks. It doesn't count *discouraged workers*. In other words, your unemployed friend who has given up trying to find work and is crashing on your couch and promising to help with chores one of these days. As well as millions of other unemployed friends crashing on millions of other couches and promising to help with chores one of these days.

The official unemployment rate doesn't count the growing population of homeless people. It doesn't count people that are *underemployed*—people that have jobs but aren't making enough to live. Perhaps you weren't aware of it, but some of those underemployed people are homeless. Because having a job doesn't mean you can afford to move out of your car.

In related news, since the strategy of "massaging the facts" (lying) works so well with unemployment, the government is considering applying it to the official homelessness rate. Homelessness will vanish when the government concludes that nobody can be homeless since the earth is our home.

POVERTY ALSO SUCKS

Directly related to the need for unemployment is the need for poverty. Rather than go into a long explanation, I'll just mention an essay I ran into recently, entitled "Is Poverty Necessary?" by Marilynne Robinson. The essay concludes that poverty is definitely necessary.

I already knew a lot of the reasons why, because they're the same reasons that make unemployment necessary. But I learned another thing that economists don't tell us about: *the iron law of wages.* You might get an economist to tell you about it if you get them drunk enough, or blackmail them by threatening to publish leaked selfies of their stimulus package.

If so, they'd tell you it means that the price of labor for a substantial portion of the population must be kept just above the level of subsistence. This is critical for the economy because, as Robinson put it, "If wages rose above subsistence, this would plunge the whole system into ruin."

HEY, APOLOGISTS FOR
OUR ECONOMIC SYSTEM,
DID YOU CATCH THAT?

If Marilynne Robinson is right (and she is), what does that do to your claim that economic growth is the solution to poverty?

ANOTHER ELEPHANT?

Sorry, we're not allowed to mention this. Sounds like another elephant in the room that we need to ignore.

SILICON VALLEY BILLIONAIRES
DO HAVE A CONSCIENCE

At least *some* of them do. Some of them have pondered the effects of the advances in artificial intelligence that their companies are responsible for. Those Silicon Valley billionaires asked themselves, "How can we justify growing insanely wealthy by developing technology that eliminates millions of jobs and pushes the entire population into debilitating financial fear?" Their reply is that the country needs to institute some version of Universal Basic Income (UBI) which ensures that every citizen is guaranteed a minimum level of subsistence income.

The idea is perhaps a noble one—that in a civilized and affluent country, no citizen should have to worry about being reduced to living in a box. Aboriginal and so-called "primitive" societies guarantee basic survival for all of its citizens. Why shouldn't it also be guaranteed by the richest and most powerful country in the world?

Well, the problem is that the richest and most powerful country in the world is addicted to economic growth. Let's say that America instituted some version of UBI. Americans would be free of debilitating financial fear. They wouldn't be forced to accept the type of horrible jobs that nobody would do if it wasn't for debilitating financial fear. If all employers were impelled to pay wages high enough to make people do jobs they don't want to do (which is pretty much *all* jobs) then economic growth would stop and the economy would collapse and the zombies would eat our brains.

So don't hold your breath waiting for UBI to ever be implemented. Our addiction to economic growth requires the presence of debilitating financial fear and prevents our "advanced" civilization from doing something that "primitive" societies accept as a basic premise of civilized people.

I THOUGHT GREED
WAS A BAD THING?

Greed is universally considered to be wrong. Yet we limit our consideration of greed almost exclusively to individual people and organizations, and fail to realize that the context in which they all function can be based on greed.

It's no secret that our economic system is dependent on greed. This was once openly acknowledged, such as in Ivan Boesky's famous statement "Greed is good." The reason that "greed is good," according to our economic system, is that if greed stops then the economy will collapse. It's because of that little "addicted to economic growth" thing that has its roots in the dynamic of interest-bearing loans.

Interestingly, the dangers of that dynamic were once acknowledged. This is where I want you to recall those religious terms from before, which I told you to remember.

"Religious terms?" you ask.

How could you have forgotten already? That was only a few pages ago.

"Are you talking about *usury* and *avarice?*"

Yes, those are the ones.

"I thought those were porn star names."

No. At least I don't think so.

"They're twins, if I'm not mistaken."

I'll check it out later. But for now I'm going to use the terms in their religious sense.

Okay, let's start with *usury*. The concept of usury, of charging interest on loans, was long condemned by organized religion. This attitude hasn't totally vanished. It has existed through modern times, at least as far as Gandhi who included the concept of "wealth without work" as one of his Seven Deadly Social Sins.

In the view of the church, to charge interest on a loan was seen as a way to profit from someone else's hardship. It was seen as a form of the sin of *avarice*—of "the excessive desire for wealth." Later, of course, charging interest on a loan became not just one aspect of the economy, but the basis of the economy. The dynamic was introduced by bankers who were definitely motivated by "the excessive desire for wealth."

Hmm... Since that sin has now become the basis of our economic system, does that mean our entire economic system is sinful? That's a very powerful idea to consider. I probably need to check with the Pope before I make such a bold pronouncement.

Here's another old-timey religious word you don't hear very much anymore: *plenitude.* It means "having enough." The idea is to be satisfied with having only what you truly need, and not be greedy for things that will blind you to what's truly important in life. The reason you don't hear this word very much anymore is because to be greedy for things that will blind you to what's truly important in life is what keeps the economy from collapsing.

Since we're throwing around all these religious terms, it's good to remember that The Bible—despite what many think—

does *not* equate money with evil. What the New Testament states, in 1 Timothy 6:10, is this:

> For the love of money is the root of all evil: which while some coveted after, they have erred from the faith, and pierced themselves through with many sorrows.

Money itself isn't the problem. It's the *love* of money which is evil—which "pierces ourselves through with many sorrows." The problem isn't money, its *greed*. An overriding focus on money leads us to see all people and all of existence in instrumental terms as means to our own personal gain. And this degradation of their dignity necessarily degrades our own. And by effecting ourselves in this way—by "piercing ourselves through with many sorrows"—we effect outer life in precisely the same way. If greed blinds us from seeing that life is sacred, then it blinds us from seeing its destruction. And that blindness creates an economic system based on greed which is equally blind.

If interest-bearing debt *within* an economy was once seen as a bad thing, then what of an economy *based* on interest-bearing debt? The only way organized religion could condemn usury now would be to condemn our entire economic system. I'll ask the Pope about this, and see if he's in the mood to condemn our entire economic system.

SORRY, BUT GETTING RID OF BILLIONAIRES WON'T SAVE US

Many people seem to believe that if we made billionaires share their wealth in some magical way (such as by taxing them) it would solve not only our economic problems, but essentially all of our problems. If only we could get rid of billionaires, they believe, the result would be a blessed land of milk and honey that's beneficial to everyone that's not lactose-intolerant or grossed-out by the idea of sweetening things with bee spit.

Yes, the level of wealth inequality in America is beyond obscene. I'm certainly not defending it. But don't hold your breath waiting for our politicians to fix it, because our addiction to economic growth won't let them fix it.

Should we make billionaires share their wealth? Sure—if we could do it in a way that wouldn't cause the economy to collapse. But even if we managed to do this, it still wouldn't solve our addiction to economic growth. But at least if we get rid of billionaires, we'll all go down together with a more equitable distribution of wealth. That's good, right?

LET'S GET RID OF
OF CAPITALISM!

Many of the same people who believe that getting rid of billionaires will solve all of our problems believe the same thing about capitalism. If we could only get rid of capitalism, they believe, nobody would be lactose intolerant or grossed-out by the idea of sweeting things made with bee spit. But to explore how much truth there is to this belief, we need to ask an interesting question.

WHAT IS CAPITALISM?

Most people define it as something like "an economic system based on the private ownership of the means of production." Some critics of capitalism focus on this aspect. But is the private ownership of the means of production necessarily a bad thing? What about Brenda's private ownership of *Brenda's Donut Shop* which has the means of producing the finest donuts you've ever tasted?

Many critics who focus on this aspect seem to believe that we could fix everything by switching to socialism. To these critics I have a response: Have you ever tried living in a socialist country? Give it a try and get back to me on whether you found utopia.

Other critics of capitalism focus on the ways in which capitalism ruthlessly circles the planet like a tidal wave leaving a trail of destruction in its wake. Okay, *now* we're getting somewhere. But such critics tend to ignore that what *drives* the destruction is our addiction to economic growth.

We could argue about whether the problem is capitalism or our addiction to economic growth. But it would be a silly argument, because we're both right. The addiction to economic growth is an integral aspect of what makes capitalism work. Before capitalism, the amount of money in circulation stayed the same. The economy could not expand. But credit—in the form of interest-bearing debt—made it possible for the economy to grow. As Yuval Noah Harari, previously mentioned as the author of the best-selling book *Sapiens, A Brief History of Humankind*, put it: "Credit brought real economic growth, and growth strengthened the trust in the future and opened the way for even more growth." Also—although it wasn't the plan—it created an economic system addicted to destruction and doomed to collapse.

If a socialist country has an economy based on the introduction of money as interest-bearing debt, it hasn't solved the problems of capitalism at all. Destruction is still necessary to keep the economy from collapsing. The only difference is that the destruction becomes directed by the government rather than by private individuals—by committee rather than by the "invisible hand."

SURE, IT'S EASY TO POINT TO PROBLEMS, BUT WHAT ABOUT SOLUTIONS?

There are strategies that could drastically reduce—or even end—the aforementioned problems with our economic system, and transform it from life-degrading to life-enhancing. ☺ Although there's not a chance in hell they'll ever be adopted. ☹

WHAT ABOUT THOSE
DARNED EXTERNALITIES?

Let's say that you're a business owner who wants to "do the right thing." You hope to be an ethical manufacturer of guillotines for the growing masses of impoverished Americans dissatisfied with the country's billionaires. So you use sustainably-harvested wood. The blades are made from recycled metal. The ropes used to raise the blade are made of organically-grown hemp. Your factory runs on clean energy and uses processes that create no toxic waste. You pay your employees well and offer a generous benefit package. As a result of "doing the right thing" your product costs twice as much as your competitors who don't care about being ethical. America's impoverished masses can't afford it, and they turn to Walmart to satisfy their guillotine needs. You are rewarded for "doing the right thing" by going bankrupt.

Let's consider the idea that the free market isn't intrinsically bad or wrong. Let's consider that the main problem is the fundamental error of ignoring externalized costs—costs which we have to pay, whether our economy counts them or not. So what we need to do is eliminate those costs. But how on earth could we accomplish such a thing?

ONE ANSWER TO THE
PROBLEM OF THOSE
DARNED EXTERNALITIES

One answer to the problem is simple—at least in theory. What we need to do is: *internalize the externalities!* Several years ago, this author learned about this solution from the book *The Ecology of Commerce* by Paul Hawken. The book proposes what some have called *green capitalism*. The basic idea is to retain the basic market system, yet modify it by forcing the producer to internalize the externalized costs. This could be done in a number of ways. But whatever method is used, the idea is that the market price reflects the full cost of the product.

Let's look at some examples related to fossil fuels. The price of electricity from coal-burning power plants would rise to reflect the health costs caused by the pollution. The price of gasoline would rise to reflect the costs of global warming and the costs of the wars to protect our oil supply.

As a result of the higher prices, sustainable energy options become economically competitive. Suburban sprawl—only feasible with an abundance of cheap gasoline—becomes prohibitively expensive, thus encouraging intelligent urban design. The same thing would apply to industrial agriculture, which wouldn't be able to compete with small-scale local farms.

Here's another example. At this point, pretty much every product on earth is totally or partially made of plastic. Which isn't great because plastic is made out of oil. And plastic waste is rapidly becoming a major environmental and health problem. But what if we required companies to internalize the costs of things made from oil-based plastic? Then it would become economically competitive to make things out of natural materials, like we've been doing for all of human history up until 100 years ago.

It's possible to make plastic out of natural ingredients, such as soybeans. If the full costs of oil-based plastic were internalized, it would be cost-effective to make soybean-based plastic. Wouldn't you rather have your money going to a soybean farmer than an oil company?

This could be applied to *everything*. Forestry. Transportation. Manicures. Yes, we could internalize the previously externalized costs of manicurists who use flagrantly unsustainable methods of providing nail care.

In such a scenario, companies would still compete for business. But they would be competing to be more sustainable. Not out of some idealistic notion to "save the earth" or "do the right thing," but to make more money.

In our current system the "invisible hand" encourages destruction. But in this system the invisible hand would work to *eliminate* destruction. Imagine two images: The first image consists of an immense hand smashing down forests; the second image consists of an immense hand gently planting seedlings.

It's an interesting idea, yes? Maybe we should consider it. It would give our economy meaning—a metaphysical foundation. Or rather, it would change the foundation from "destroy life" to "affirm life." If we decided to base our civilization on the idea that the meaning of life is to "leave the world better than we found it," then this would align our economy with that idea.

Unfortunately, there would be some significant challenges involved in implementing such a system. Perhaps the biggest challenge would be figuring out the costs of the externalities. If the creation of a product resulted in pollution or released carcinogens, how much should be added to the cost of the product? This sounds extremely difficult to the point of being impossible.

IS THERE A SIMPLER WAY TO
GET RID OF EXTERNALITIES?

Yes there is! It's very simple: *Don't allow them.* Eliminate the costs of pollution by banning pollution. Eliminate the costs of carcinogens by not allowing companies to produce carcinogens. Ban all externalities! Problem solved, easy-peasy!

SOUNDS GOOD, BUT...

Such strategies could conceivably do some good things, such as sustaining life on earth. But it doesn't take a rocket scientist to figure out that getting rid of externalities—either by internalizing them or banning them—would mean that prices would go... *which way?*

That's right, they would go *up!*

One problem with this is that so many people are living on the edge that an increase in prices would mean even more people moving into boxes. There are ways in which we could resolve that problem, such as having people who can afford multiple homes share some of their money with those who can only afford boxes. There are also ways that we could drastically lower the cost of housing. (To be explored in the next chapter.) There are a variety of ways that we could create a society in which we didn't need as much money, and could focus instead on enhancing our quality of life.

But there's a deeper issue that would prevent us from developing a life-affirming economy. The economy must grow—the Money Pit Junkie Monster must be fed. Eliminating externalities wouldn't result in economic growth; it would result in the opposite of economic growth. Which, for an economy addicted to growth, wouldn't work out too well.

A SOLUTION TO *THAT* PROBLEM

So we would also have to deal with that nagging little problem. But guess what? We could! Recall that that the source of the problem is the creation of money by banks in form of interest-bearing loans. But it doesn't have to be that way. And historically speaking, that's not how it was supposed to be.

It's a little-known fact that—per the intention of the United States Constitution—Congress is meant to have the power to issue and control the nation's money. But less than two years after the adoption of the Constitution in 1791, the United States officially put itself under the control of private banking by legitimizing debt-based money as the only legal currency. It did this with the enactment of the First National Bank Act—a move engineered by Alexander Hamilton and the international financiers he represented.

Perhaps, gentle reader, you enjoyed the musical *Hamilton*, and sometimes find yourself humming some of the inspiring and catchy songs. Unfortunately, the musical didn't really explore the implications of what Alexander Hamilton's actions did to America. If it did, you'd probably quit humming those songs.

Because as a result of Hamilton's actions, just as America was beginning its great experiment in political freedom, it made itself economically dependent. Mayer Amschel Rothschild, founder of Rothschild International Bankers, once boasted: "Permit me to issue and control the money of a nation, and I do not care who makes its laws." (I'm pretty sure that while he was saying this he was laughing fiendishly and twisting his evil moustache.)

By now the situation is accepted in America, but at the time it was seen by some as a great danger. In a letter to John Taylor, Thomas Jefferson wrote:

> I believe that banking institutions are more dangerous to our liberties than standing armies. Already they have raised up a money aristocracy that has set the Government at defiance. The issuing power should be taken from the banks and restored to the Government to whom it properly belongs.

So what's the solution? Was Jefferson on the right track? Should the issuing power be taken from the banks and restored to the Government to whom it properly belongs?

YEAH, JEFFERSON WAS ON THE RIGHT TRACK

We just need to make sure we do it in a way that ends our addiction to economic growth. This is how this author would put it: *Stop the addiction to economic growth by ending the introduction of money as interest-bearing loans. Discontinue the fractional-reserve system, and put the Federal Reserve under the control of the Treasury, with the exclusive right to issue currency free of debt.*

Here's the interesting thing: A couple of presidents actually tried this. A couple of presidents actually attempted to defy the big banks.

The first attempt was Abraham Lincoln's creation of 450 million dollars of debt-free Constitutional money called *greenbacks*. The money was printed and entered into circulation as official U.S. currency.

Isn't that interesting? I used to think the word *greenbacks* was nothing more than slang for *money*. Little did I know!

Anyway, Lincoln's idea ended up not working out too well. The greenbacks were depreciated and bought up by financial speculators, who later forced Congress to redeem them for gold. Also, Lincoln was shot in the head.

The second attempt was by President John F. Kennedy. Not too many people know about Executive Order 11110. It was similar to what President Lincoln tried. It took the power to create money away from the private banks, and gave the Treasury Department the power to create debt-free money. Some of the money even got printed while President Kennedy was alive. But the money disappeared, shortly after Kennedy was shot in the head.

I'm not really a conspiracy theory person, but I find it interesting that the only two presidents who seriously challenged the big banks were shot in the head. So if there's a president out there who wants to attempt this again, I strongly recommend wearing a thick helmet and not going outside too often.

THAT WOULD BE THE EASY PART

But the implications would not be easy; the implications would—

WAIT! THAT WOULD BE THE *EASY* PART?

Yes, which is one of many reasons I've concluded that we're doomed. Because there's no way in hell we'll even *consider* the easy part. Now, to continue...

But the implications would not be easy; the implications would require fundamental changes to every aspect of our society. The changes that would be required are beyond the scope of this book. They're beyond the scope of mainstream economists, whose focus has almost exclusively been on getting more as opposed to how to live well with what we've got.

But some have dared to venture into this new and unknown terrain. Probably the most well-known is economist Herman Daly, author of books such as *Steady-State Economics* and *Beyond Growth: The Economics of Sustainable Development*. Economist Kate Raworth has devoted her career to the question: "How can we turn economies that need to grow, whether or not they make us thrive, into economies that make us thrive, whether or not they grow?" Many people are working on similar questions. Several organizations are devoted to the topic, such as the Center for the Advancement of the Steady State Economy, The International Society for Ecological Economics, and the Post Growth Institute. A lot of information is out there, waiting for us to realize that we need to take it seriously.

I greatly admire these folks, and feel sad that nobody is paying attention to their efforts to save us from collapse. I wish them well in their efforts to avoid suicidal depression.

Let's end this chapter on a positive note. The sale at Taco Bell is still in effect! But this is the last day. So if you want to get an additional Chicken Gordita for the same price you would have paid for it anyway, get in your car and drive as fast as you can to Taco Bell. Burn up some fossil fuels. Since nobody else worries about externalities, why should you?

CHAPTER 5

WHY CAN'T I BUILD A HOME THAT'S IN HARMONY WITH LIFE?

We explored how the metaphysical foundation of our economic system is not entirely positive in the sense that it has resulted in a system dependent on the destruction of life and is based on a pyramid scheme that's doomed to collapse.

Could it be that other aspects of our civilization are based on the same metaphysical foundation? Could it be that this also results in the destruction of life? Could it be that this author can't think clearly because he's out of coffee?

The answers are *Yes*, *Yes*, and *Oh no!*

This author will continue on to the next paragraph after a quick trip to get more coffee.

Getting coffee right now...

...Okay, I'm back.

As for how other aspects of our civilization are based on the same metaphysical foundation, it would take an outrageously long chapter to explore them all. But you, gentle reader, surely have no desire to read an outrageously long chapter exploring them all. And this author surely has no desire to write an outrageously long chapter exploring them all.

So rather than explore all those aspects, I'm going to focus on one of them (with brief mentions of some other ones). I'm going to focus on the concept of *home!*

Home... Shelter from the elements, a roof over our head. And hopefully walls to hold the roof up.

Home… Where we share so many precious memories and television commercials.

Home… Where every year we mark the height of little Tabitha to chart her growth. Unless little Tabitha has one of those weird "shrinking diseases" and is getting littler.

Home… Where each night we lay down our weary head after drinking too much cheap wine, which explains why our head is weary.

Home… Otherwise known as "home sweet home." Or possibly "apartment sweet apartment." Or maybe "box sweet box."

One reason that America's "living in a box" lifestyle is growing in popularity is because housing costs have been rising faster than incomes. As a result, it's increasingly difficult to afford a home. There are statistics that clearly indicate this trend, although I can't seem to find the exact figures at the moment. But according to the statistics, fifty years ago *(a big number)* percent of people were able to own a home. But now, only *(a small number)* percent are able to own a home. The trend is undeniable. Figures do not lie.

TODAY'S YOUNG PEOPLE
ARE WELL AWARE OF THIS

Once again, I feel very bad for you, young people of today, who don't expect to be able to afford your own homes. Once upon a time, owning your own home was accepted as something that all little boys and girls could look forward to. It was an important landmark in the process of growing up and becoming boring.

You know that you'll never be able to afford to own home. But what you don't know is *why*. The reason is that literally every aspect of society is opposed to it.

In order to understand this non-life-enhancing dynamic, we need to explore the concept of *paradigms*.

WHY SHOULD I GIVE A DAMN
ABOUT THIS PARADIGM THING?

Honestly, I wish that whoever is writing these section headings would take their job a little more seriously. But anyway...

The reason we should "give a damn about this paradigm thing" is because paradigms form the basis of our individual and collective lives. Physicist and systems theorist Fritjof Capra defined a *paradigm* as "a constellation of concepts, values, perceptions, and practices, shared by a community that forms a particular vision of reality that is the basis of the way a community organizes itself."

The term *paradigm* is synonymous with terms such as *pattern of beliefs* or *underlying philosophy* or *overriding perspective* or *worldview*. It's synonymous with the concept of a *metaphysical foundation*, described earlier regarding economics, in which everything about our culture is built upon "our basic outlook on life, its purpose and meaning."

If you're at a party and are trying to describe the concept of a paradigm to somebody, you can just keep throwing out these terms until you find one that sticks. But if you're trying to describe the concept of a paradigm at a party, it sounds like it's not a very fun party. Or it sounds like you're not really a party person. (The definition of a *party person* is "someone who doesn't try to describe the concept of a paradigm at a party").

The thing is, whether you have any idea of what a paradigm is—or what it consists of—we all have one. You can't deny it. If you try to deny it, you're denying it on the basis of your paradigm. There's no escape. Rather than deny you have a paradigm, why not spend that energy figuring out what your paradigm is? It can be a lot of fun. Be the first in your neighborhood to host a party with the theme: "Let's figure out what our paradigm is."

Sorry, but I can't make it to your party. Whatever day your party is going to be, I'm busy that day.

Actually, we have more than one paradigm. We have a personal paradigm of individual beliefs, contained within a shared social or cultural paradigm—consisting of the beliefs and qualities that make a collection of people American or German or Navajo. And there are sub-cultures within those cultures—overlapping paradigms that shape and influence each other in fascinating ways, which you'll discover at your party.

If you're interested in exploring this in more detail, I highly recommend the book *Patterns of Culture* by Ruth Benedict. I'm pretty sure bookstores offer discounts on multiple copies for paradigm parties.

Cultures have always needed paradigms. A stable society depends on the majority of its individuals following spoken and unspoken rules, and moving within a range of acceptable channels. Such channels, once defined by simple tribal principles, evolved to become modern society's complex regulatory laws and codes, and the rules of its financial and economic systems. A paradigm results in a system of values and ethics as a result of a simple formula: What fits the paradigm is good; what doesn't fit the paradigm is bad. A paradigm includes taboos, or "elephants in the room": questions forbidden to ask because the answers would be a threat to the integrity of the pattern.

A paradigm determines answers to existential questions. If our idea of a meaningful life is to leave the world better than we found it, then what's our definition of "better"? Your Uncle Jeremy the corporate CEO defines *better* as whatever leads to less government regulation. But your Uncle Martin the professor defines *better* as anything that crushes the corporate class and leads toward a revolution of the proletariat. Your dad defines *better* as freedom from marital obligations. Your mom—hurt that her husband defines *better* as "freedom from his wife's needs"—reacts by defining *better* as "finding a better husband."

A CLASH OF PARADIGMS

We tend not to notice our paradigm when surrounded by others who share it. For example, if you're a skateboarding punk rocker vegan anarchist hanging out with other skateboarding punk rocker vegan anarchists, there's a sense of belonging that comes from being among people who share the same views. Everything's cool.

But let's say you're a left-wing bisexual performance artist from Chicago. If you find yourself surrounded by a group of right-wing fundamentalist frat boys from Tallahassee, you'll experience *a clash of paradigms.* Another way to say it is *culture shock.* Another way to say it is *getting beat up by a group of right-wing fundamentalist frat boys from Tallahassee.*

Let's say you're one of those right-wing fundamentalist frat boys from Tallahassee, and you decide to visit the isolated Oowanga tribe deep in the forests of Borneo. Why do you wish to do this? Because you're a sensitive and caring right-wing fundamentalist frat boy from Tallahassee. You feel the Oowanga culture lacks something they need, and you want to help them obtain it.

Even if you'd survived, they probably wouldn't have been too excited about your idea to create a major league football team called the Oowanga Eliminators. They probably wouldn't have been able to relate to your paradigm, which includes the idea that it's desirable to build a massive stadium in which groups of men chase a ball made of pigskin. They might, however, have been interested in chasing an actual pig. Not for sport, but to catch it and roast it over a fire.

Different paradigms! Different ideas about what's good and valuable versus what's stupid and batshit crazy.

The reason you didn't survive is because of what happened when you were introduced to the chief. Your version of an appropriate greeting—a slap on the back and a hearty handshake—was the gravest insult possible. According to the Oowanga's paradigm it was a flagrant invasion of personal space which was interpreted as an act of war. If you had survived to read these words, you would now understand that what you experienced was *a clash of paradigms.*

EXCUSE ME, BUT YOUR
PARADIGM IS SHOWING

Paradigms not only shape our attitudes; they also shape our cultural landscapes. When we look at any aspect of human civilization, we see the raw materials of nature shaped in particular ways. We see energies channeled into specific directions to suit particular purposes. And all this shaping and channeling is done by paradigms.

This isn't mystical woo-woo talk—this is *science!* The field of archeology is based on the premise that the artifacts of past civilizations—the physical forms they left behind—reflect the ideals of those civilizations. Ancient Greek architecture such as the Parthenon reflected the ideals of Western rational thought. Other types of architecture reflect other ideals.

Since our paradigm is everywhere, it's invisible. Everything we see is an expression of it. We can't see it because we're surrounded by it. There's a metaphor related to this, about how fishes are unable to comprehend the concept of water because they're continually swimming in it. I know this is true because I once spent an afternoon trying to explain the concept of water to a trout.

Which leads us to ask a very important question: *What's our paradigm?* As far as I've been able to discern, the foundation of modern civilization consists of several interrelated ideas. The core idea is:

Humanity is separate from and superior to nature and other forms of life.

Other ideas are corollaries:

Moral concerns don't apply to interactions between humanity and nature. Nature is merely raw material without intrinsic value.

Ethics are based on rights rather than responsibilities.

The individual is primary. Society is secondary at best, and a distracting illusion at worst.

Only what can be measured is real. Existence consists only of parts.

Nothing is sacred—or alternately, only churches and religious texts are sacred.

Progress is defined in material terms of consumer possessions, technological ability, and economic affluence.

Economic value is equal to social value. Questions of worth can be answered based on profitability. What encourages profit is good. What opposes profit is bad.

That's our paradigm. More specifically, it's the paradigm of Western Civilization—the dominant civilization on earth.

To people in other cultures, such as the isolated Oowanga tribe deep in the forests of Borneo, our paradigm is literally insane. And I'm not the only person in our very own culture to agree with the isolated Oowanga tribe deep in the forests of Borneo. Perhaps you, gentle reader, having our paradigm revealed to you for the very first time, agree with us. Perhaps you have a sense that basing an entire civilization on such a paradigm could be... oh, let's say, *problematic.*

CONSPICUOUSLY ABSENT

Let's consider some of the things that are *not* included in our paradigm. Does it include *wisdom?* Nope. How about *sustainability?* No, I don't see that one, either. What about *becoming more deeply aware of how life is an interconnected whole and learning how to live in harmony with it?* Sorry, none of these are part of our paradigm. So they must not be important.

CONSEQUENCES

Let's pretend we're doctors. We're diagnosing our symptoms to discern the underlying disease. Let's look at some symptoms: resource depletion, global warming, pollution in the air, toxins in the air and water.

None of these are "side effects"—a term we use as a form of denial, as a way to feign surprise. *Gosh, we poured poisons into the ground and atmosphere, and somehow they ended up in our food and water.* The symptoms are direct consequences of specific actions, which are a direct result of our paradigm.

Why is there air pollution and global warming? Is it because of industrial smokestacks and internal combustion engines? Yes, superficially. But why are there industrial smokestacks and internal combustion engines? It's because we want things that require industrial smokestacks. It's because we want the benefits and conveniences made possible by internal combustion engines. It's because of pursuing things that our paradigm declares to be good.

Seen in this light, with some idea of the disease, we examine a civilization that is now *full* of symptoms.

A 165-WORD PRE-EMPTIVE RANT
IN RESPONSE TO PEOPLE WHO ARE GOING
TO ARGUE WITH ME ABOUT THIS

Some people put all the blame on the companies operating the industrial smokestacks and producing the internal combustion engines (and the gasoline that does the combusting). However, these deluded people somehow overlook that MILLIONS OF PEOPLE WANT THE THINGS CREATED BY THE COMPANIES AND GIVE THE COMPANIES MONEY FOR CREATING THEM.

Sure, we see a photo of a factory with a huge pipeline dumping millions of tons of toxic sludge into our favorite swimming hole, and get mad at the company that owns the factory. But if you follow that sludge upstream to what caused it, you'll find that it leads to the products in your very own kitchen, and to the kitchens of all your friends, and to the kitchens of millions of people who might like to be your friend if only you'd give them a chance. You might be pleased to discover that they're decent people, if you got to know them, even though they're responsible for the microplastics that are killing you.

HOW DOES OUR PARADIGM
RELATE TO THE RISING
COST OF HOUSING?

We've already covered quite a bit of territory on how paradigms determine our cultural reality. In fact, I'm considering using that information to produce a series of overpriced seminars to be called *The Power of Paradigms*™ that you can't afford to miss. *Call 1-800-PARADIGM to reserve a spot alongside others also hoping to discover the variety of ways that ideas shape their lives.*

Now, let's explore how our paradigm applies to the concept of *home*. Specifically, let's see how—

Wait a minute, a cowboy is heading this way, riding a horse. And he doesn't look happy.

"Just hold on one goldarn minute! Society isn't based on ideas. Society is based on *facts*, on hard realities. I'm not governed by ideas. I'm the master of my own fate!"

How free are you, really? I'd say that you're free only within limits that you had no choice in creating. Are you free from the effects of our addiction to economic growth? Are you free from the forces that are outsourcing jobs and driving wages down? Are you free from the rising cost of housing which is making it increasingly impossible to afford a home?

"Well, I don't know much about that. But I know for sure that I'm free to stop listening to your bullshit so I can ride through the range off into the sunset."

Farewell, cowboy and good luck. May wealthy developers not buy the range and arrest you for trespassing.

Now, where was I?... Oh yeah. I was going to explore how our paradigm is related to the rising cost of housing.

OH, BY THE WAY...

Here's a little digression "just for fun." Keep in mind that in order to own a home it's necessary to own the piece of land on which it's built. Let's briefly consider the question of whether we should be required to pay money to occupy a portion of the planet on which we were born and from which we are literally made. Shouldn't that be some sort of "natural right"? Why do we have to earn our right to occupy the planet?

No other species except humanity does this. For example, bears don't have to pay for what other bears describe as "a quaint hillside cave, perfect for hibernation." But if they did, here's an example of a business card that would be used by a bear that specializes in selling caves to other bears:

BOB THE BEAR
Licensed Realtor

Address: Meadow near headwaters of Pine Creek
Contact: Go to meadow and yell, "Hey, Bob the Bear!"

Okay, that's enough playful irreverence. Let's move on to something a bit more serious.

IT'S TOTALLY POSSIBLE TO BUILD HOUSING THAT'S AFFORDABLE

Children and foolish idealists occasionally ask a ridiculous question: If we want more affordable housing, why don't we simply build more affordable housing? It isn't impossible; there are many ways to construct modest homes at a fraction of the price of the oversized and unaffordable monstrosities that are the only options society gives you.

Perhaps you've heard of the *Tiny Home Movement?* In case you haven't heard of it, this is a movement that advocates for small homes that can be constructed for a fraction of the cost of a typical home. Unfortunately, throughout the country they're either heavily discouraged or banned outright.

Don't worry, there are other options. There are all sort of manufactured homes—not just the old-fashioned mobile homes that have a less-than-positive reputation among many people. Some of them are really cool! Unfortunately, throughout the country they're either heavily discouraged or banned outright.

As for those old-fashioned mobile homes, they're getting harder to find since mobile home parks have been steadily eliminated for the past several decades. There are still a few left, in places where they're grudgingly allowed because they're located in places where a substantial number of people live on the edge of poverty. Local governments are leery of banning them, since this would push the residents into homelessness. Including, in some cases, the people who run those local governments.

Occasionally a developer (foolishly, idealistically) approaches a city council with a proposal consisting of something like, "Hey, I can build modest housing for half the cost," and the response (translated from official city council legalese) is essentially, "Don't let the doorknob hit you on the way out."

In order to understand all of this, we now return to the exciting topic of *paradigms*.

LET'S BUILD A
LIFE-AFFIRMING HOME!

If you *really* want to experience the power of a paradigm, just try defying it. Let's consider what would happen if you tried to build a modest and inexpensive home designed to exist in harmony with life.

This author has dreamed about building such a home for years. It would be compact and incredibly energy-efficient, insulated with walls made of straw bales. The walls would be sealed with cob—a mixture of soil and straw that's reminiscent of adobe. The home would be constructed of locally-obtained materials, and would be designed and oriented to take advantage of solar heat in the winter and cooling breezes in the summer.

Solar panels would take care of most or all of the humble electric needs.

The yard would consist of an organic garden and mini-orchard, thereby providing fruits and vegetables from right outside the window—as opposed to the current outrageous waste of food travelling over a thousand miles from farm to kitchen.

IMAGINE THERE'S NO MORTGAGE, IT ISN'T HARD TO DO

We could build such a home for a fraction of the cost of a "normal" home. It would require less materials, and those materials could be obtained relatively inexpensively. Labor costs would be vastly reduced, or maybe even eliminated. The design would be simple enough to be built by non-professionals, so we could do most or all of the work ourselves—or by inviting friends and family to join us in a home-building party. We would provide pizza and beverages, of course, because that's the kind of people we are. But not beer. Because having a bunch of drunk people build your home might not work out too well.

Such a home would abandon the current "normal" requirement of wage slavery for two people for 30 (or more) years of their lives for a home that's overpriced to begin with, even before the interest on the mortgage inflates the cost by tens of thousands of dollars.

Imagine the implications if we could choose such an option. Freed from paying an outrageous mortgage, we could devote less of our lives to work, and more of our lives to life. We would have more time for vacations, for creative pursuits, for family, for volunteering for worthy causes, for contributing to our community.

By greatly reducing its environmental impact, such a home would affirm life. And by being incredibly affordable, it would also affirm the life of its owners. So the modest and inexpensive home designed to exist in harmony with life would also affirm *human* life.

WHAT A GREAT IDEA!

We're supposed to be free, so why not allow people the freedom to pursue such an option, right? People don't *have* to live in such a home. If people want to live in an overpriced monstrosity, they can. But if people want to live in a something different, that should be okay, right?

The only problem is that it would be fiercely opposed by every aspect of society. Here's what would happen:

- The banking and finance industry would lobby against any attempt to allow or encourage such homes.

- They would be joined by every Homebuilders Association, developer, lumber company, and business associated with the building industry.

- Need we add that the entire Real Estate industry would be opposed?

- The neighbors would rise in opposition.

- The government would never allow it

But how could this be? The lack of affordable housing is a big problem, and so is environmental destruction. Modest ecological homes would help solve both problems. Shouldn't they be... oh, I don't know... *encouraged* or something? Instead of being fiercely opposed?

Where shall we begin untangling this web of irrationality, this apparent conspiracy against something we should be encouraging?

BUILDING CODES

Our laws are expressions of our paradigm. Laws are the rules by which a society encourages what it considers to be good, and prohibits what it considers to be bad. Our laws can be thought of as the enforcer of our paradigm. The police officer that arrests you for *breaking the law* is actually arresting you for *subverting the paradigm*.

This brings us to consider building codes, which are the laws that determine what kind of homes can be built. Some people believe (mistakenly and hilariously) that building codes are to ensure safety. The reason that this belief is so mistaken (and hilarious) is because there's absolutely no reason to believe that smaller and less-expensive homes are any less safe than the expensive monstrosities you see going up in suburban housing developments.

Maybe you don't want to live in something "different" like a tiny home or straw bale home, but just want to live in a "regular" home that's small and efficient?

Sorry, that's not allowed.

Perhaps you didn't know that building codes generally include a *minimum size restriction*. In other words, it's against the law to build a small home. In addition to size, another way the codes enforce expensive homes is with specifications that require industrially-produced (expensive) materials and specialized (expensive) methods. Affordability and ecological integrity are not only discouraged, they're explicitly banned. A modest and inexpensive home designed to exist in harmony with life is against the law.

Let's repeat that and put it in italics because it's kind of important: *A modest and inexpensive home designed to exist in harmony with life is against the law.*

FOLLOW THE MONEY

As for why business interests are against something we should be encouraging, their opposition is simple to understand. It would mean less money for them. What would the banking and finance industries think of homes so inexpensive that building them would require only minor loans—or no loans at all? As for real estate and construction interests, it's obvious where their money comes from.

All these business interests would automatically condemn the idea, regardless of the benefits. Believe it or not, business interests sometimes care less about improving society than about maximizing their own profit. As for the idea that building codes are designed to ensure safety, I'll concede that this is true in the sense of ensuring the safety of that profit.

By comparison, the only entity that benefits from affordable housing is people that need housing. Which is pretty much all of us, actually. *But wait…* That includes the neighbors. And according to this author, the neighbors would rise in opposition. What's up with that, author?

WHY ARE THE NEIGHBORS AGAINST AFFORDABLE HOUSING?

The opposition from the neighbors is interesting. Why should they care if somebody wants to live next to them in a modest and inexpensive home designed to exist in harmony with life?

Let's pay a visit to the hypothetical neighbors. Let's call them *Rob* and *Laura*, after America's favorite couple from *The Dick Van Dyke Show*—arguably this country's first great sitcom. Imagine them living in a typical suburban home, with two lovely children and a minivan that can haul the whole gang to weekend soccer games—including their dog *Skippy*, named after America's favorite peanut butter.

Imagine that I'm constructing my dream home next door. When Rob and Laura take a look at it, what do they see? What do they think of it?

Our paradigm determines whether what we see is "good" or "normal" by a simple criterion: *Does it fit the paradigm?* So Rob and Laura's opinion of the home will be based on whether it fits the paradigm that produced *their* home. It would be the paradigm that produced every home they've ever seen, including every home they've seen their favorite television characters live in.

That paradigm dictates that a home should be tidy, respectable, and orderly—based on Euclidean geometry of planes and right angles. It dictates that a home can be made of any material found on earth, as long as it's sold by a building supply company. The paradigm dictates that colors should be muted. No pink or orange or neon purple. Murals of butterflies or gnomes are definitely unacceptable, because that's the kind of thing done by hippies. And the paradigm dictates that they don't like hippies.

The yard, like the home, should be tidy, respectable, and orderly. It should consist mostly of a lawn, which shouldn't be allowed to grow over the straight edge of the sidewalk. Nobody can explain why, but everybody agrees that it would just be *wrong*. The lawn should be kept green and well-trimmed. Dandelions are to be considered a mortal enemy, no matter that they're beautiful, and that the flowers and leaves are edible, and that the roots can be used for medicinal tea. It's okay to put poisons into the ground to kill them.

A few shrubs are okay. The shrubs should be respectable shrubs and, like the lawn, be kept well-trimmed. Decorative plants are preferred. Plants that actually produce something useful—fruit, vegetables, building materials—should be discouraged.

Ecological realities are to be ignored. There's no need to use local sources of building materials, or to adapt the home to the climate. The home is expected to look basically the same whether it's built in Alaska or Arizona. There's some degree of flexibility, because individual expression is extremely important in America. There's total freedom over which muted color to paint the home, and over which shrubs are planted in the yard—as long as they're tidy, respectable, and orderly

The home should be a reflection of the homeowners, who should also be tidy, respectable, and orderly. They should be invested in the American Dream and all it implies and entails. They should care about who wins the Super Bowl. If they don't care about who wins the Super Bowl, they *better* care about who wins the World Series.

In other words, if the home is expected to be boring and unoriginal, then the same expectation applies to the homeowners.

HELLO, NEW NEIGHBORS! WHAT DO YOU THINK OF MYAFFORDABLE ECO-HOME?

When Rob and Laura gaze upon the curious new home being built by the curious new neighbor, the doubts begin. They notice the walls being insulated with something that's not pink fiberglass. They notice that the angles aren't perfectly square, and the walls aren't perfectly flat. And what's that stuff he's using to seal the walls? Is that...*mud?* And what was it he said about getting rid of the lawn and replacing it with...*a garden?* When Rob and Laura discuss the situation, their doubts become verbalized as: *How can we stop this thing?*

Perhaps the skeptical reader thinks I'm exaggerating? Not at all. People have reacted like that over far less. Tearing up a lawn and replacing it with a garden has been enough to inspire lawsuits and calls to law enforcement agencies to eliminate the threat.

Years ago I came across an article by Nicols Fox entitled "The Clothesline Question: How hanging out the laundry sparked a political firestorm." It tells the story of what happened when our hapless protagonist innocently began hanging laundry in the backyard when her clothes dryer broke. She was surprised to discover that this had a variety of benefits. Such as avoiding the cost of a new dryer. Such as cutting down on her electric bill. Such as becoming better attuned to the natural world.

But when the general public discovered what she was doing, the attacks started. She was declared to be "sanctimonious" and "self-righteous." She was accused of insulting people forced by poverty to hang their clothes because they can't afford a dryer.

As a cigar is not just a cigar, a clothes dryer is not just a clothes dryer. For some people rejecting a clothes dryer is rejecting the whole idea of progress. It's not quite bringing us back to the Stone Age, but it's bringing us back to the more recent Clothesline Age.

In conclusion: What would Rob and Laura see if I tried to build my modest eco-home next door? They would *not* see a home in harmony with life. They would see an outright danger. They would see a threat, a rat-infested jungle, a hazard to hygiene, a breeding ground for God-knows-what. They would see an affront to decency, tidiness, and order—a cheap home of sticks and mud, an insult to—

CHEAP?

Wait, did someone say *cheap?* Why should that matter? Why can't somebody decide what they want to pay to put a roof over head, whether ten million dollars or ten thousand?

Because (now we're *really* getting to the heart of the matter) according to the paradigm of a home accepted by Rob and Laura, a home is more than just shelter from the elements. It's also an *investment*. Because a home is so expensive (since inexpensive options aren't allowed) it's the largest financial investment most of us will ever make. Therefore, when those fortunate enough to afford a home gaze upon it, one thing they see is a *retirement nest egg*. (Imagine an enormous egg stuffed with thousand-dollar bills.)

If my modest eco-home is built next door to Rob and Laura it will not only insult their sense of decency and goodness. It will also insult their investment by depressing property values.

And what might they be thinking of the curious new neighbor who's destroying their retirement income? Perhaps their internal dialogue runs something like this: *We didn't put up with 30 years of jobs we hate just to see the payoff wiped out by some hippie who wants to tear up the lawn and grow their own beans!*

If we weren't such a civilized culture, Rob and Laura would band together with the rest of the neighborhood and descend at dusk with torches and pitchforks to burn down my home and run me out of town. But since we *are* civilized, we'll just let the government do it.

WHY IS THE GOVERNMENT
AGAINST AFFORDABLE HOUSING?

Consider that local governments are funded primarily via property tax revenues. Ask yourself: Is the government going to propose legislation for affordable housing that would vastly reduce those revenues?

While you're pondering that...

We also need to consider the effect that affordable housing would have on economic growth, which we're addicted to. Anything that contributes to a simpler, less materialistic, less expensive lifestyle is bad for economic growth. So to sustain our addiction to economic growth (which is an expression of our paradigm) we've created building codes (which are another expression of our paradigm) that require our shelter take the form of a large (oversized) and costly (way too damned expensive) home. This is important for the economy because it forces us to make a substantial amount of money for one of the most basic and necessary aspects of existence. Modest and inexpensive homes designed to exist in harmony with life can't be allowed, because if the idea caught on in a widespread way the economy would collapse.

As a result of her experience with the clothesline, Nicols Fox became aware of the larger implications of what she was doing: "I realized that a line stretched across the backyard had the potential to undermine assumptions the economic system depends upon."

THE PROFIT MOTIVE

Let's say that when Rob and Laura think about retirement, they aren't satisfied with simply getting their investment back (adjusted for inflation, of course). They want to sell it for *more*. In other words, they want to make a *profit*. Lots of people have this same idea. They think it's natural to think this way. Nobody seems to even question it. Well, let's be "different" and question it, okay?

Let's consider "D." I should mention that "D" is a person that this author knows personally, but wishes to refer to anonymously because this author doesn't like getting yelled at.

I had a nice little chat with "D" recently. She explained that she bought her home 20 years ago for $50,000, and it's currently appraised for $600,000. She expects that when she retires it should be worth around $800,000. That worked out really well for "D"! A $50,000 investment that will soon be worth $800,000.

But wait... What about the next generation? ☺ for "D" but ☹ for the next generation. And ☹☹ for the generation after that. Because to keep this up, each generation must pay more for housing, taking an ever-increasing proportion of overall income.

When "D" told me about the huge profit she plans to make on her home, I commented *in a polite and respectful manner* about the next generation having to pay oh-so-high prices for housing. Guess what she said? She said, "Oh, it's a real shame."

I didn't say it out loud, but I wondered whether "D" felt it was enough of a shame to do anything to remedy the situation. Such as being willing to sell her home for less money. Such as lobbying the city to make affordable homes available for people that don't happen to have access to $800,000.

Making money this way places an undue burden on future generations by making housing less affordable in an attempt to provide retirement income for a succession of previous generations. It's an investment scheme in which an increasing debt is passed on to future investors.

THAT SOUNDS FAMILIAR...

That reminds me of something from earlier in this book. That sounds very similar to...

Hey! I know what it is!

It's another pyramid scheme—just like the pyramid scheme of the overall economy, with each player gambling on getting their winnings before the game collapses.

Hmm... Is a real estate system like this—that profits by siphoning wealth from future generations—guilty of the sin of *avarice*? I'll add this to my list of questions for the Pope.

ANOTHER ELEPHANT?

Sorry, we're not allowed to mention this. Yes, it's another elephant in the room that we need to ignore. It's getting really crowded with all the elephants in here. Maybe we need to move them into the backyard?

STUCK IN THE MIDDLE WITH YOU

We're caught in the middle of two addictions, two pyramid schemes. Recall that the addiction to economic growth works toward paying people as little as possible. Now, combine that with the other pyramid scheme—the addiction to rising real estate prices—which works toward making housing as expensive as possible.

You may have noticed that both of these addictions work toward the interests of "the powers that be." The rest of us are being squeezed in the middle, and many of us are being squeezed out entirely.

Once again, I feel very bad for today's young people. If you're one of today's young people, you're very aware that you're being squeezed in the middle. You've basically been squeezed out before you even had a chance to squeeze in. So I guess you've been pre-squeezed?

SOLUTIONS THAT AREN'T

But don't worry, because "the powers that be" are working on solutions. The main solution proposed by the "powers that be" is, of course, more economic growth. Don't make homes less expensive; make increasingly expensive homes affordable with the promise of eternal economic growth forever and ever. This isn't working, of course, but don't count on "the powers that be" to mention it.

But there's another proposed solution, which is somewhat extraordinary and quite surprising. This author has seen—over and over—a very peculiar proposal toward making housing more affordable. The solution is: *Increase the supply of unaffordable housing.*

HUH?

This so-called "solution" is being actively applied in many cities, such as Portland, Oregon. To some people, such as children and foolish idealists, this sounds a bit *counterintuitive*. But it's perfectly sensible, we are told by rational grown-ups: It's a matter of *supply-and-demand.* If we create a surplus of unaffordable housing, then other housing will start to become affordable. In other words, by building housing that only wealthy people can afford, affordability will trickle down to the rest of us.

This sounds a lot like the myth of trickle-down economics. This myth doesn't work, either. This myth has been officially debunked.

I'm referring to a recent article in *Oregon Business* magazine, which estimates that 16,000 rental units in Portland remain vacant. Yet the city continues to encourage the construction of huge housing complexes—huge *expensive* housing complexes.

Has this helped with affordability? According to *Oregon Business*, it has! ☺ But only by 2.2 percent ☹ According to my (very accurate) calculations, for the average Portlander that's about enough for a monthly treat of a pizza and a six-pack of tall boys.

And there's some other information that just came to light. That not-too-impressive 2.2 percent reduction was concentrated at the luxury end of the market. Which means that the solution to create more affordable housing for low-income people actually created more affordable housing for the wealthy.

If you imagine that this revelation has caused the city to realize that the myth is bogus, then you're either a child or a foolish idealist.

HERE COMES A RANT

I explored earlier how we're surrounded by symptoms of our paradigm. We see them. We smell them. We hear them.

As for hearing them... A symptom that especially bothers this author is related to those tidy, orderly, well-trimmed lawns. Imagine, if you will, the following scenario: It's a pleasant summer afternoon. And since it's a pleasant summer afternoon, might as well open the windows and let some fresh air in. It would be an excellent time to relax and listen to an album of classical guitar recordings by Ana Vidović, a musician from Croatia who is—

NNNRRRRRRRR!!!

Oh no! That's the neighbor starting up the lawnmower. Which will be followed by the edger. Which will be followed by the weed-whacker. Maybe in an hour or so this author can listen to the album in peace. Unless the other neighbor starts up their mower.

If you suspect that this author is not amused, you're absolutely right. I don't just feel distracted. I feel assaulted. The noise bothers me doubly because it's more than just noise. The dissonance is philosophical as well as audible. I'm hearing a paradigm in action, a reminder of the underlying mindset of society. When I hear a lawnmower, I'm hearing refineries making gasoline to power millions of tiny engines spewing noise and pollution to sustain something that's absolutely unnecessary.

Once the weed-whacker has finally stopped, all is quiet except for the gentle *whoosh* of a broom to clean off the sidewalk, right?

No.

Because why do something quietly with an inexpensive tool when it's possible to use a gas-powered blower to do it loudly while adding more pollution and burning more fossil fuels.

Recently I came across some fun statistics. There are 40 million acres of lawn in the United States. Mowing this much lawn burns 800 million gallons of gas per year, which causes over five percent of urban air pollution. Also, homeowners use up to 10 times more chemicals per acre on their lawns than farmers use on crops, which ends up in our drinking water and waterways.

And this is legal. Perfectly acceptable.

Why? Because it's all supported by the assumptions of our paradigm. In a sane society, it would be seen for the insanity that it is.

GRASS IS PEOPLE, TOO

In case you missed the point, I don't like lawns. I could go on and on, counter-rebutting your rebuttals until you give up.

Do you know what's crazy? Maintaining a lawn is a pain, but if you ask people why they have a lawn, they don't know. Generally the answer is, "Because everyone else has one." But if you ask everybody else, they don't know either. This is an excellent point to bring up to people who claim that they're self-directed rational beings who aren't governed by a paradigm they had no choice in creating.

Some people explain their reason for having a lawn as something like, "I like to look out the window and see some nature." My rebuttal to that is: A LAWN IS THE MOST UNNATURAL EXPRESSION OF NATURE THAT CAN POSSIBLY EXIST.

Allow me to explain. (And sorry for yelling.)

Or actually, let's allow a lawn to explain. That's right, this book is going to do something no other book has ever done: It's going to give voice to a lawn in order to let us know what we're putting it through.

I must warn you, gentle reader, that this is emotionally-challenging stuff. Get out those Kleenex in case you start getting teary-eyed.

To convey the personal and heartfelt nature of the following essay, this author is going to set the text in a very personal and heartfelt font called *Lucinda Calligraphy*.

~ ~ ~

AN OPEN LETTER
TO HUMANITY

I'm a lawn. I'm an unnatural monocrop of a genetically-identical grass variety, forced together in unnaturally close proximity. Imagine if one of you—let's say, Donna from accounting whose favorite band is Duran Duran—was forced to live packed next to other Donna's from accounting whose favorite band is also Duran Duran.

Doesn't sound like much fun, does it?

But the weirdest thing about how you treat us is the mixed messages you constantly send us. Because one day you'll be feeding us with fertilizers and watering us to make us healthy and green. But the next day, you bring out those horrible machines. As we're trying to grow tall, to make you proud of us, you cut us all down!

Do you love us or hate us? Just imagine you were a lawn, and somebody was doing this to you.

Someday I'd like to make a family. You know, swap pollen with another grass plant—hopefully a cute one—and form seeds. In other words, to go through the normal life cycle of maturity, then procreation, then abandoning this mortal coil as my offspring carry on without me to repeat the same cycle.

But you won't let me do that. You won't let me grow up. You won't let me embrace my role in the cycle of life. As you won't let me die, you won't let me live.

Remember the Golden Rule. It works for humans. It also works for lawns.

~ ~ ~

Gentle reader, I hope that wasn't too emotionally devastating. Perhaps, after hearing from a lawn's perspective, possibly for the first time in your life, you'll relate to lawns a bit differently. Perhaps you'll "see" lawns differently than before. Perhaps your paradigm of lawns (and by extension, of all existence) will be irrevocably altered.

WHO'S THE BOSS?

Consider this: We're a nation of 330-million-or-so people, on a planet of several billion people, scurrying around on our daily round of activities, functioning more-or-less as a cohesive whole. I know that I'm not the only one to consider all this and then wonder: *Who's in charge?*

Because *nobody* is in charge. Not really. Certain people are in so-called "positions of responsibility," but they have little power to fundamentally change anything on their own.

Who do we blame for outlawing my affordable eco-home? We can't really blame the individuals enforcing the law. They're just doing their jobs. "It's nothing personal," says the building inspector who condemns it. And the police officer who arrests me for building it. And the demolition crew that tears it down.

We're held within the constraints of the law. But what is *the law?* It's the enforcer of what we define as right and normal—it's the enforcer of the paradigm. So the solution, ultimately, is to change the paradigm.

But who's responsible for the paradigm?

Everybody. Nobody.

It's obvious that humanity is heading toward self-destruction. But nobody is doing it purposefully. Nobody is saying, "Well, if our goal is to destroy ourselves, this is the way we should do it." Each of our choices appear to be perfectly normal and completely rational, consistent with past choices and aligned with the overall course of history. There's nowhere we can go to confront it. There's no "center" where it's coming from.

In an essay about the Middle East, Sue Kutz wrote about the demoralizing "atmosphere of powerlessness" she encountered there: "'The Situation' is what everyone calls the state we're in. It's a depersonalized term that reflects the feeling that there is no one responsible and no control possible."

This perfectly describes our situation. Individuals come and go, but the assumptions we collectively base our civilization upon are adopted and perpetuated by succeeding generations.

From this point of view, it's the paradigm's fault.

Sometimes it appears obvious that the problem is the fault of the government. But as long as we live in a democracy, we have the power to change the government. Or maybe the problem is the fault of the economic system. But if the economic system needs to change, there's nobody to change it besides us.

So back to the question: Who's in charge? The answer is: *The paradigm is in charge. But we're in charge of the paradigm.*

How hopeful. And how depressing.

Hopeful because all we have to do is collectively embrace a life-affirming paradigm and the tangible results will follow. It could happen tomorrow. There's not a single physical thing stopping it. *Depressing* because the chances of it happening make a snowball's chance in hell look pretty good.

We've become accustomed to winning at the expense of life. What will it take to give up the idea of winning? What will it take for us to realize that this false win makes us both lose? If the impending collapse of human civilization isn't enough, then what is?

I have an idea. As far as I can tell, people in America only listen to pop stars. What if a major pop star released a song that encouraged us to change our paradigm? It would be a catchy dance tune, of course, and the chorus would be something like, "I think it's about time / To change our paradigm." There would be a music video, of course. I'm envisioning a montage of scenes of death and destruction, with the pop star shaking their head and making a pouty "I don't approve!" expression. This would be followed by a montage of scenes of living in harmony with life, with the pop star smiling and giving a big "thumbs-up."

Yeah, it probably wouldn't work. But do you have a better idea?

CHAPTER 6

IF ADDICTION IS A BAD THING, THEN WHY IS OUR CIVILIZATION DEPENDENT ON IT?

Why did we base our civilization on an insane paradigm? Good question! Well, nobody sat down and figured out the paradigm and said to everybody else, "Okay, we're basing our civilization on *this*." We didn't consciously formulate our paradigm. It's just what made sense to us. It was the cultural expression of what felt right. It was the outer reflection of our internal state of being.

Perhaps you've noticed that our paradigm appears to be *egotistical?* That's because it is! Our paradigm is an expression of the ego. In order to understand this very important point, we need to explore the role of the ego within the evolution of consciousness.

YOU KNOW THAT CONSCIOUSNESS EVOLVES, RIGHT?

Of course you do. If you're reading this book, it's a sign that you're an intelligent and highly-evolved person. But you might have to explain it to your unevolved friends. You might have to explain that each civilization had its own unique cultural evolution, but this accompanied an overall psychological evolution that broadly applied to humanity as a whole. You might have to explain that the way in which consciousness evolves throughout the life of an individual person is a microcosm of how consciousness has evolved throughout human history. Or as you frequently find yourself saying, *Ontogeny Recapitulates Phylogeny*.

You might have to explain to your unevolved friends how human culture has evolved through four broad stages. Those stages were described by social philosopher Jean Gebser as archaic, magic, mythic, and mental—which correspond to the human developmental stages described by cognitive psychologist Jean Piaget as sensorimotor, preoperational, concrete operational, and formal operational. And you might have to explain the effects of these psychological stages on civilization, as was explored in the book *Up From Eden; A Transpersonal View of Human Evolution* by Ken Wilber.

And if you can get your unevolved friends to understand all this, you can explain that it means that they're evolving!

THE EGO IS BORN

The emergence of self-consciousness or self-reflective consciousness deserves special attention. For consciousness to reflect upon itself there needed to be a self to do the reflecting. Therefore, the emergence of self-reflective consciousness was accompanied by something new and unprecedented: the ego, the skin-encapsulated self, the individual "I."

Before that emergence, we didn't experience ourselves as individuals. A pre-reflective "group mind" internalized collective beliefs which were unquestionable because there was no "I" to question them. Events before this time were "prehistoric" because there was no individual self that was capable of reflecting upon events through time.

HELLO IT'S ME

It's amazing to consider that at some unknown historic moment, approximately 6,000 years ago, the first person was able to conceptually become separate from the world—to realize that they were an individual person. Which is something that we all go through. Over time, every child becomes increasingly able to differentiate themselves, and at some point re-experiences that historic moment when they realize their separateness from the world. Some people remember that moment. This author is one of those people.

At about the age of two or three we begin to use the word "I" before we comprehend its meaning and implications. The study of ancient literature has revealed the identical process occurring in cultural evolution. And both personally and culturally, our evolution continues in comprehending the meaning and implications of the word "I."

CONTINUING THE JOURNEY

Surely evolution hasn't stopped with us—with the average John and Jane Doe that you see at the 7-Eleven drinking razzleberry-flavored Big Gulps before hurrying home to watch the new episode of *Celebrity Babysitting*. Surely this isn't the pinnacle of evolution.

If we continue the journey, where will it lead? This brings up a series of related questions. How do we define an *evolved* or *well-adjusted* person? How do we define *mental health?* How do we define what's *sane?*

Sigmund Freud had a theory. His *reality principle* held that sanity was adjustment to reality, with *reality* defined as the status quo of the surrounding culture. Yet when World War I began and he witnessed jubilant citizens rushing off to die by the millions in muddy disease-filled trenches, he questioned whether an entire culture could be less than sane.

And honestly, have we gotten any saner since then? Have we evolved? I'm not talking about technological evolution, such as televisions that allow us to watch *Celebrity Babysitting* in higher resolution. We could question whether a culture consisting of jubilant citizens rushing home to watch *Celebrity Babysitting* is less than sane.

The attempt to define a healthy person led psychology to consider individuals whose focus has gone beyond adjustment to society, beyond meeting basic needs and achieving a healthy sense of self-esteem. It led to "self-actualized" individuals whose perspective has widened beyond the skin-encapsulated separate self. Our early life consists of developing a healthy ego—of a healthy sense of individual identity. Further development consists of expanding that identity beyond the individual self—beyond all varieties of tribal, racial, and national identity—to discover a common identity with all humanity. And beyond that, with all life.

Which leads us to consider the individuals that are widely considered to have achieved something like human perfection. They're the ones who say crazy things about how all of existence is a living expression of an undivided whole, and that the goal of life is to love one another.

Wouldn't it be nice if everybody based their lives on crazy things like that? Wouldn't it be nice if we based human civilization on crazy things like that? As for why we don't, that's something we'll explore later.

WHAT IF WE DON'T EVOLVE?

The important thing to realize is that we're not just our ego. The ego is a stage to be outgrown—to be evolved beyond. Kind of like how an obnoxious teenager has to evolve beyond that snotty "the world revolves around me" attitude. Actually, *exactly* like that. Because that's exactly how the ego is.

Consider that we have a word for people who act exclusively from their ego. That word is: *egocentric*. And in common everyday experience, we know that such people do things that aren't very nice. Acting exclusively from our ego makes us do things that, if you were a Boy Scout or Girl Scout and did those things, you would *not* get a merit badge or achievement patch.

Here's a short list of some of the things that the ego does. This list is the result of years of careful study, involving real-life incidents in which this author was personally involved. Think of it as a shopping list for the ego, a to-do list of what needs to be done to fully realize the negative implications of the separate self.

If you're a spiritually-minded person, you can think of it as a *not-to-do list*. You can think of it as a laundry list of all the dirty stuff that needs to be washed from the soul in order to give it that quality of spring-like freshness. Here are just a few things that the ego does. The problem with the ego is that it...

...rushes into crowded elevators before giving other people a chance to get off.

...runs the lawnmower Saturday at 7:00 a.m. when everybody's trying to sleep in.

...secures a barking dog outside the coffee shop, then runs off somewhere for an hour while their barking dog annoys everyone at the coffee shop.

...tailgates six feet behind other cars at night with the high beams on. *And possibly...*

...flashes those high beams as a signal to pull over when there's clearly no place to pull over.

...leaves lousy tips. Or worse, demands special service: "I know I sent this omelet back once already to substitute mozzarella cheese for cheddar and to remove the onions that I forgot to tell you I'm allergic to, but I decided I'm in more of a 'pancake' mood now." And then *doesn't tip at all.*

...makes a phone call, then puts the other person on hold. *And speaking of phones...*

...carries on loud cell phone conversations in public places like buses and libraries, forcing everybody to listen to such fascinating tidbits as "Oh, not much, just sitting on the bus," or "Oh, not much, just hanging out at the library."

...asks, "Hey, could you help me a couple hours on Saturday morning?" for a task that, due to lack of any preparation whatsoever, takes the entire day and night.

...sits quietly at a meeting, allowing a co-worker to take the rap for their mistake.

...corners someone at a party, backs them into a wall, and traps them into listening to a dull, rambling, monologue without a break. *Hours later, this kind of jerk...*

...remains the final guest at the party, staying long after everyone else has left, and is totally oblivious to the host's exaggerated yawning, frequent watch-checking, and repetition of the statement "Well, it's getting late..."

...waits until evening in the campground, when everyone else is back from the day's adventures and peacefully relaxing around campfires, to start up the gas-powered generator.

...impels tall guys in the audience at a concert to rush to the front of the stage just when the band starts, forming a six-foot-tall biological fence that blocks the view of everyone behind them.

Of course, I'm not the first one to realize that the ego has problems. The negative qualities of the ego were recognized thousands of years ago, as far back as Ancient Greece, when Aristotle referred to the ego as an *igbay atfay erkjay*.

THE EGO: PROS AND CONS

All of this has led many to interpret the ego as *bad*—as a thing to be resisted or subdued. But this is a mistake. To declare war on the ego is just as bad as glorifying the ego. Because we can't function without an ego. A healthy ego is an integral aspect of being a psychologically healthy person.

Seen in the context of evolution, the ego was an inevitable development. Consciousness could only become self-reflective with a self to do the reflecting. That's fairly obvious, isn't it? Or to put it another way, the ego is necessary as the aspect of consciousness required for consciousness to live in time. That really doesn't need to be said, though, since *everybody* knows that.

The problem is the illusion that we are the ego. Our task, therefore, is to get rid of the illusion, not the ego. The process isn't one of subduing or stifling the ego, but expanding it; not becoming less than an individual, but becoming more than an individual.

A CONCISE SUMMARY OF THE PSYCHOLOGICAL EFFECTS OF BEING TRAPPED IN THE EGO WHICH INCLUDES A SEGUE TO THE TOPIC OF THIS CHAPTER

If we live exclusively from our ego is doesn't just result in being a jerk to other people. It leads to being a jerk to ourselves. In fact, that's the aspect that many people focus on. The ego is considered to be problematic by psychologists as well as by the world's wisdom traditions. The ego keeps us out of touch with reality, creates unrealistic expectations, and gives us an undeserved sense of entitlement. Being trapped in the ego is to become trapped in an illusory sense of self which traps us into pursuing illusory and impossible goals. The ego interferes with our ability to genuinely love others. It leads us to live in a way that damages ourselves, which results in damage to those around us. It leads us to act from the most superficial and self-centered part of ourselves, the aspect that succumbs to greed, envy, and all the other negative aspects of being human. Including... *drum roll, please...* addiction!

THE ROOTS OF ADDICTION

Buddhism is especially helpful in understanding all of this. The essence of Buddhism can be summed up as something like this: Suffering (*duḥkha*) is the result of the kinds of attachment that result from being trapped in the ego, and the way beyond suffering is the process of moving beyond the ego. In *Buddhism: A Way of Life & Thought*, Nancy Wilson Ross describes the emotional trap of the ego:

123

Man, by his unwillingness to accept what he interprets as life's failure to give him, without stint, whatever he desires, finds himself caught in an emotional trap of his own making. This trap is the product of his ego. It takes form from the self's insatiable appetites and delusions, its enormous blind unattainable desires, its never-satisfied craving or thirst, *tanha* or in Sanskrit *trishna*. It is *tanha* which leads the individual to place a tacit demand on life which life by its very nature cannot fulfil.

If that sounds like addiction, that's because it is. Addiction is an attempt by the ego to find meaning where it can't be found. It distorts us by steering us toward superficial answers to life's deepest questions.

TO BE CONTINUED
AFTER A BRIEF NOTE

Sorry about the sexist language in the quotation by Nancy Wilson Ross. I decided to retain the quotation as-is, rather than convert it to gender-neutral terminology—a decision that applies to all the quotations used in this book. At the time it was written, everybody wrote as if they were sexist jerks—even women!

NOW, WHERE WAS I?

Sorry, I'm having trouble keeping track of the narrative. I'm writing in a coffee shop, and I think I've had too much coffee. Also, there's a Bob Marley song playing.

Speaking of coffee, here's a tip. If you order a hazelnut latte, it will generally be flavored with what's called "hazelnut flavoring syrup" which may contain little or no actual hazelnut. But consider that *Nutella* consists of actual hazelnut butter (with the addition of cocoa to make it extra delicious).

Bring a jar to your favorite coffee shop (I'm assuming you've already established a mutually-beneficial working relationship with your barista) and have them add a heaping tablespoon to your latte. Delicious! Don't forget to tip your barista generously.

GET BACK TO THE
POINT, AUTHOR

It's not really my fault—the scattered narrative. It's the coffee. I was doing fine until the coffee was consumed.

A NOTE FROM THE EDITOR

Hello, I'm the editor of this book. It was my responsibility to make some kind of sense out of the mess that the author gave me. You think this is bad? You should have seen it before I got out the red pen!

I'm just popping in here for a quick second to point out that the author is trying to manipulate you with a cheap literary trick. Did you notice how he constructed that last sentence? He wrote, "I was doing fine until the coffee was consumed." That's called *passive construction*. It's meant to take the responsibility away from the author and blame the coffee. As your editor, please allow me to give responsibility where responsibility is due, and convert the sentence to *active construction*. What the author meant to say, if he had any integrity or self-respect, is: "I was doing fine until I consumed the coffee."

Well, I hope that was enlightening. I'm going back to my desk, where a bottle of rum will open.

OKAY, BACK TO
WHERE WE LEFT OFF

The topic of addiction is very important. Not only to your local bar that counts on alcoholism to stay in business. It's also important when considering why human civilization is collapsing and we're all doomed. But for now, let's consider the question: Why are there so many bars? Or maybe it's more relevant to ask:

WHY GET DRUNK?

Alcoholism has been called a "liquid cosmology," and addiction a "misguided urge for wholeness." At the heart of addiction is a craving for a certain kind of experience, for a *high*—a temporary transcendence, a temporary escape from the trap of the separate self. Remaining in this trap results in a type of psychological pain referred to as *angst* or *malaise*. Psychologist Viktor Frankl called is the *existential vacuum*.

But the high of addiction isn't the kind of natural high achieved in moments of transcendent unity—moments in which we simultaneously lose ourselves and find ourselves. The high that motivates addiction is superficially similar yet fundamentally different. It's an unnatural high in which we don't find ourselves, we only temporarily lose the part of us that we're trying to escape.

THE AUTHOR IS VERY
FAMILIAR WITH THIS

This author would like to explain his presence at Darwin's Theory last night, for two hours, drinking three beers. Actually, it was three hours, and four beers. But who's counting, other than the bartender? The point is, this author was not there to escape the pain of existential angst or malaise. He was there to share in the convivial exuberance of a bunch of half-drunk people making fun of stupid movies.

Okay, maybe this author was there to escape the pain of existential angst or malaise a little bit. Maybe five percent. But who's counting, other than the bartender?

WHAT'S THE DIFFERENCE BETWEEN
THIS AUTHOR AND A RAT?

The answer to this question is: *Not much*. People and rats have much more in common than you might imagine. For example, we can both become addicted. And for both of us, the cure for addiction is the same. Since we're both expressions of life, why would we expect otherwise?

This author came to these conclusions as a result of reading about some fascinating scientific experiments in an article entitled "Filling the Void," consisting of an interview with Bruce K. Alexander—a psychologist specializing in addiction research.

In the interview, he explained his skepticism about the results of studies that showed how rats can become addicted. Those studies consisted of rats that were isolated in small cages and provided with a lever they could press to access morphine or other drugs. The rats would self-administer the drugs to the point where they would stop eating.

As a result of the studies, the researchers concluded that rats have no resistance to addiction—that they're natural-born addicts just waiting for the right drug to come along. This led the researchers to conclude that if rats becomes addicted to drugs, the only cure is to take away the drugs. Which led them to consider that the conclusions regarding small mammals (rats) might also apply to large mammals (people).

But Alexander wasn't so sure about those conclusions. He noted that rats are social creatures (just like people) and they don't like being isolated in small cages with nothing worthwhile to do (just like people). If you were trapped in such a situation, wouldn't you pull the lever? I'm pretty sure I would, and I bet you would too.

So Alexander designed another experiment. The drug lever was still there, but the rats weren't isolated. They were kept in groups in what he called "Rat Park"—a pleasant setting in which they were allowed to express themselves creatively with tiny banjos, had access to Netflix, and could order pizza as long as it wasn't after 10:00pm.

Just kidding. Actually, "Rat Park" consisted of a large en-closure with play areas where the rats could romp around together. And they could order pizza at any time, even after 10:00pm. The results of this revised experiment were extremely interesting. When the rats were given access to morphine they used it only occasionally and didn't become addicted.

As a result of this experiment, we can conclude that rats (and people) aren't just a bunch of helpless addicts who can't resist a drug lever. We *can* resist, even if the lever is right in front of us. And what gives us the ability to resist?

BEING ALIGNED WITH LIFE.

Mice allowed to lead fulfilling lives according to their genuine natures rejected the drugs offered them. And that's what works for people, too.

That's what works for Bruce K. Alexander who, in the interview, shared how the conclusions of the experiment resonated with his own life. Because he once struggled with alcoholism. His recovery involved a change to a more meaningful career and to living in a more community-minded setting. According to Alexander, "I found belonging, identity, meaning, and purpose, and the alcoholism went away, just like that."

All of this was confirmed by something I heard in a TED talk by Johan Hari: "The opposite of addiction is not sobriety. The opposite of addiction is connection." Of course, not just *any* connection will work. It must be *meaningful*.

But what does that mean? What makes a connection *meaningful?*

MEANINGFUL CONNECTION™

I gave this concept a trademark because I can probably make some money with it. I'm proud to announce the concept of *Meaningful Connection*™ which you can learn about through another series of overpriced seminars. *Call 1-800-MEANING to reserve a spot alongside others also hoping to achieve a Meaningful Connection*™.

This is *brilliant!* People will flock to my seminars like gullible sheep, thinking that *Meaningful Connection*™ means to have a great sexual hook-up. Or perhaps the gullible sheep—sorry, I mean *valuable participants*—will think that *Meaningful Connection*™ means a long-term relationship, perhaps leading to marriage and a magnificent ceremony with well-wishers encouraging them to have some fun before the divorce. Sorry, I mean *encouraging them to begin their blissful journey together*.

To be perfectly clear, the concept of *Meaningful Connection*™ is all about love. It's just not about love in the personal sense. It's about love in the transpersonal sense, the sense that the Greeks called *agape*.

To refresh your memory, since you weren't paying attention in class, here's a recap of the four ancient Greek conceptions of love, including the views of each conception regarding spanking:

EROS: Passion, physical longing. The kind of love that, unless you want to have kids, involves birth control devices. Spanking is a definite possibility between consenting adults who want to add a little "spice" to their relationship.

STORGE: The kind of love between friends and siblings. The kind of love parents feel for their children. Spanking is allowed only by parents as a form of what they call "tough love."

PHILLIA: An affectionate, warm, and tender kind of platonic love. Does not include spanking, since it contradicts "affecttionate, warm, and tender."

AGAPE: An unconditional love that sees beneath the surface of each person and strives to love them as a human being. This kind of love sees the act of loving as its own reward, and expects nothing in return. If spanking happened, the administrator of the spanking would not expect a spanking in return.

It is, of course, this final and most noble and "higher" form of love—*agape*—that we're talking about here. It's about love as defined by cultural anthropologist Ashley Montagu:

Love is that form of behavior that contributes to the healthy development of both the lover and the loved. By healthy development is meant the increase in the capacity to function as a totally harmonic person who confers creatively enlarging benefits upon all with whom he comes into association.

How is this related to the idea of *Meaningful Connection*™? Because this is precisely the kind of connection that's meaningful. As for the people who sign up for my seminar, hopefully they won't be disappointed to discover that the seminar focuses not on sex or marriage, but on developing the capacity to function as a totally harmonic person who confers creatively enlarging benefits upon all with whom they come into association.

The initial seminar starts soon, call now to make a reservation. The seminar will be "all inclusive" which means that alcoholic beverages will be provided, via a lever. But don't worry, because if the seminar does what it's supposed to do, you'll resist that lever as easily as you'd resist walking off a cliff.

REVISITING RAT PARK

As a result of his experiment, Alexander doesn't view addiction as a disease. He sees addiction as an illness that's a *response* to a disease. As this author sees it, that disease would be something like *separation from a meaningful connection with life*. This is similar to Alexander's interpretation, in which he sees addiction as a way of adapting to the alienation and disconnection produced by modern, westernized society. Or as this author would put it, a society that's out of touch with life. If there's anybody out there that disagrees with this author's assertion— that thinks our society is in touch with life—I have a reply for you: *Hahaha!*

WHAT ABOUT THE WORLD?

As I wrote earlier, the ego is considered to be problematic by psychologists as well as by the world's wisdom traditions. But something critical has been overlooked. The problem is generally viewed only in personal terms: Living our lives based on the ego isn't good for us. It traps us into pursuing illusory and impossible goals. It interferes with our ability to genuinely love others. It leads us to live in a way that damages ourselves, which results in damage to those around us.

But what does living our lives based on the ego do to the world? If living exclusively out of the ego makes us act like a jerk to other people, does it make us act like a jerk to the world?

FINALLY THE AUTHOR GETS BACK TO THE QUESTION OF WHY WE BASED OUR ENTIRE CIVILIZATION ON AN INSANE PARADIGM

Which leads us to reconsider how our cultural paradigm is the outer expression of our state of being. Because our paradigm isn't based on reality. It's based on greed. Our cultural paradigm is the collective expression of the ego. It's a self-serving paradigm, created by the ego for the benefit of the ego. It's a paradigm based on the assumption of superiority that makes us entitled to take without returning, and to continually want more of everything regardless of the consequences. And since the ego considers this to be *normal* or *right* (and not insane) the ego considers a cultural paradigm based on it to be *normal* or *right* (and not insane). The reason that our paradigm conspicuously excludes things like wisdom and sustainability is because those things oppose the ego.

And as the ego effects life by placing "a tacit demand on life which life by its very nature cannot fulfil," so does our paradigm. But before we explore this idea in more detail, let's consider a topic that might describe how a reader is responding to this book.

BOREDOM

This author would like to examine another facet of addiction: as a response to boredom. But as living beings within a living universe of endless variety and infinite possibilities of expression, how could we possibly be bored?

DO YOU FIND EXISTENCE TO BE BORING?

Apparently a lot of us do. Here's a fun fact: The average American spends more than two hours a day on a smartphone. This author is unsure whether such activity qualifies as being engaged with life. This author is seriously considering making the bold assertion that checking our Instagram feed, tracking how many "likes" our Facebook post received, and re-posting comments on X (formerly known as Twitter) is *not* being engaged with life.

I can imagine that when one of those average Americans sees a post consisting of a meme that says *"The meaning of life is to live each day to the fullest"* they click "like" then go back to playing Candy Crush Saga and doing an internet search for "hot hairstyles for people standing around staring at their smartphones."

Also, the average American spends five hours a day watching television. This author is really close to making the bold assertion that this is not being engaged with life. Unless it's with a bar full of half-drunk people heckling the programs.

But here's this author's favorite fun fact about boredom: If people are given a choice between painful electric shocks and being bored, many of them will choose the painful electric shocks. According to an article from *Science* magazine:

> In 11 studies, we found that participants did not enjoy spending 6 to 15 minutes in a room by themselves with nothing to do but think, that they enjoyed doing mundane external activities much more, and that many preferred to administer electric shocks to themselves instead of being left alone with their thoughts.

Many years ago (before smartphones) Blaise Pascal wrote, "All of humanity's problems stem from man's inability to sit quietly in a room alone." Does that sound totally outrageous? Maybe so, but if you explore the full implications of that statement, you'll see that Pascal has a point. Because boredom isn't a trivial problem. It's an existential problem at the core of the human condition. It's a sign that we're not engaged in life, a sign that we're trapped in the ego.

This author is reluctant to share his views on the metaphysics of time. Partly because it's a large and complex topic which would distract from the main theme of this book. But mostly it's because who the hell is interested in the metaphysics of time? Suffice it to say that this author agrees with the words of Plato: "Time is the moving image of eternity." I only bring this up because one aspect of the metaphysics of time is deeply relevant to the topic at hand.

Boredom is a problem of time, a problem of being trapped in linear time apart from eternity. The metaphysical solution is, as Jiddu Krishnamurti put it, "the ending of time"—not by stopping it, but by transcending it. Or in other words, by ending our exclusive identification with it. Which means ending our exclusive relationship with our time-bound selves.

Failing this, our solution becomes not the endeavor to end time, but to *kill* time—to engage in superficial and meaningless activities, to keep busy at all costs, to treat silence as an enemy to be conquered.

But this can't work, since it's avoiding the roots of the problem. It's another form of addiction. It's a false solution to boredom that only keeps us entrapped in the cause.

WHY DO PEOPLE SO STRONGLY RESIST BEING LEFT ALONE WITH THEIR THOUGHTS?

Anybody that has attempted meditation knows why people so strongly resist being left alone with their thoughts. Here are some of the surprising realizations you will have, in roughly this order:

- Your mind consists of a bunch of monkeys screaming at each other.

- It was really stupid what you said at that party 12 years ago.

- You are an insignificant phenomenon in a tremendous universe that's larger than your limited mind can possibly imagine.

- You really shouldn't have thrown away that coupon.

- Everybody that has ever "liked" one of your social media posts is going to die.

- Also, you're going to die.

- Now those monkeys are throwing poop at each other.

If you persevere and get through all that, you'll eventually reach a calm center—a place of inner peace that's beneficial to mental health and well-being, a place you won't want to avoid by giving yourself painful electrical shocks. But it's really hard and takes sustained effort for a long time, so instead let's find ways to kill some time.

LET'S GO SHOPPING!

One way of killing time is the phenomenon of *recreational shopping*. This distorted attempt to resolve the division between time and eternity is the source of a type of addiction called *consumerism*.

Consumerism has its source in a kind of inner poverty that remains no matter the degree of outer affluence. Shopping covers it up for a little while. But soon the underlying boredom resurfaces. Therefore, we need more. As with all addictions, the solutions are temporary and need to be applied more strongly— a larger quantity, a bigger fix. Expectations shift endlessly upward—within an individual lifetime and over generations.

It's hard to believe, in modern America, that once-upon-a-time an orange was a rare treat, a delicacy. Of course, now we've got orange juice coming out of our ears. (Metaphorically speaking, except for people who drink way too much orange juice.) And for those of us bored with plain old regular orange juice, you can purchase many exciting variations of orange juice combined with other flavors in endless variations. Personally speaking, this author is waiting for the introduction of bacon-and-eggs-with-hash-browns orange juice, with a complete breakfast in each glass.

We've quickly become accustomed to a lot of things that were once considered to be incredible luxuries. The span of time between something feeling like a decadent luxury and feeling like it's an absolute necessity has been decreasing lately, but as of this writing it's approximately 12 minutes. And any hint of any of it being taken away brings feelings of utter deprivation, of regression, of "Going back to the Stone Age."

If we observe shoppers in a big-box superstore or major grocery store, it's obvious that they're bored. They're bored while surrounded by things that would have seemed like luxuries to medieval kings. For a few dollars, a modern shopper can purchase a mango from Hawaii, a kiwi from New Zealand, and a chocolate bar from Switzerland. A medieval king couldn't do that.

I have a question for the bored shoppers: *You have the ability to easily access more things than a medieval king, and you're still not satisfied?* Here's another question I could ask: *What would it take to make you satisfied?* But there's no need to ask, because I know that the answer is: *nothing*. Because that path will never lead to that destination.

LET'S RELATE THIS TO A
BIT OF SOCIAL HISTORY

The consumer society began in America in the 1920s, when economists and business executives grew concerned that our rising industrial productivity would soon meet people's basic needs. Their fear was that the American people—fulfilled at the material level—would quit shopping and focus their energies on loftier and more meaningful goals.

The appropriate response to their fear is: *Hahaha!* Their fear might have sounded like a sensible concern at the time, but apparently those economists and business executives weren't familiar with the concept of *tanha*. Because of the ever-expanding desires of the ego, they had nothing to fear. Because the public took to consumerism like fishes to water. (Sorry, I can't come up with a more original metaphor.) But business executives didn't know this at the time. Thus began the age of advertising. In other words, the creation of artificial needs through mass marketing.

Oh—did I say *the creation of artificial needs?* I meant to say *informing the public of needs they didn't realize they had.*

The definition of "basic needs" expanded as expectations continually shifted upward, and continue to do so. We expect to have more than our parents, and our children to have more than us. Failing to achieve this seems to break a law of nature.

Which is a fine line away from the truth. The idea of each generation being better off than the last isn't bad. In fact, it might be the "meaning of life"—if you subscribe to the crazy idea that we're supposed to leave the world better than we found it. Yes, each generation is supposed to be more *something*. But not more affluent, not owners of more things. How about each generation being *more wise, more enlightened, more informed, more intelligent, more closely aligned with life?*

"Sorry," replies the American public, "we'd rather have a bigger television and a more expensive car."

OUR INTERNAL ADDICTIONS
BECOME EXTERNALIZED
IN THE PHYSICAL WORLD

We shouldn't be surprised that our psychological additions become externalized as physical addictions. If you're surprised by that, I really don't know what to say. How could you possibly be surprised by that?

We already explored our addiction to economic growth, which we can think of as psychological greed externalized into an economic system based on greed. Which is directly related to consumerism. The desire for endless economic growth makes consumerism possible and depends on it to continue.

Which brings us back to the question of what living our lives based on the ego does to the world. Does it make us act like a jerk to the world? The answer is: *Yes*. If our collective need consists of *more of everything*, then who or what pays the price for that need? According to the dictionary, *to consume* means "to destroy, to spend wastefully, to squander, to use up." This is precisely what consumerism does to the physical world. It places a "tacit demand on life which life by its very nature cannot fulfil."

There are many, many, many, many, many examples, but this author will explore only a few of the most important ones. That way, you won't have to yell, "Okay, author, we get the idea! We don't need any more examples!" You won't need to yell at this author, because this author has very considerately taken the step of pre-yelling at himself. You can thank this author by making a charitable tax-deductible contribution to his bar tab.

LIFE REQUIRES ENERGY

Earlier, while exploring the issue of Peak Oil, this author related the fun fact that the source of essentially all energy on earth is the sun. Energy stored as fuel is a result of photosynthesis—the biochemical process by which a plant uses the sun's energy to create complex compounds that can be broken down or "burned." The process, broadly speaking, is called *oxidation*, and is used in our own bodies to break down fuel, or "food," into the energy that makes it possible for us to dance like crazy when a James Brown song is playing.

Until the industrial revolution, humanity's use of energy was limited to the output of the local ecosystem. Energy was stored and transferred in vegetables and grains, in animal feed, and in firewood. Our industrial age was made possible by tapping into the energy of the sun stored in fossil fuels. By tapping into this energy we were able to ignore the sustainable output of our annual "solar budget" by releasing millions (or is it billions?) of years of stored sunlight in a few generations. Every day we burn 27 years of stored solar energy. This could possibly be considered to be unsustainable. One reason we could possibly consider this to be unsustainable is that oil is starting to run out.

What should we do? Surely we can retain our current lifestyle by switching to an alternative source of energy. That's all we have to do, right?

ADDICTIVE THINKING

To demonstrate how addictive thought processes work, let's have a conversation with someone that has a "Save the Earth" bumper sticker on the car they drive to Whole Foods to buy organic gummi bears and free-range peanut butter.

Hi there, are you worried at all about oil running out?

"No problem! When oil runs out, we can grow fuel with crops such as soybeans or corn."

Well, the problem is we're using pretty much all our arable land to grow food. There isn't close to enough productive land to grow enough fuel to meet our current energy needs.

"No problem. We can switch to solar and wind power, and replace all our gas-powered cars and trucks with electric vehicles."

Well, the problem is that to replace the energy provided by fossil fuels we'd need, according to a recent study, 3.8 million wind turbines and 90,000 solar plants. The cost of building and maintaining all this would be exorbitant, and would mean living in a landscape of energy installations that would cause a variety of problems.

"No problem, we can build more hydroelectric dams."

Well, we've already put dams on nearly all the rivers of the world. In addition, dams have limited lifetimes because they fill up with silt. Over time, there will be fewer hydroelectric dams— not more.

"No problem, we can go back to burning wood to generate steam-powered electricity."

That won't work, because deforestation is already a problem. Therefore we don't have enough wood.

"Um... nuclear?"

Sure, if you want to live with growing stockpiles of radioactive waste contaminating our environment and causing cancer and birth defects, and increasing the chances of more deadly accidents such as occurred at Chernobyl and Fukushima.

"Well if it comes down to it we can always go back to riding horses, right?"

Only if you tell me where all the hay would be grown to feed the horses, since essentially all the productive land is already being used to grow food. And in addition... Hey wait a minute, come back!"

"Sorry, I've got no time for your pessimism."

There's no need to be pessimistic! All we have to do is reduce our energy needs so we can live within sustainable limits.

"Oh right! You want us to go back to the Stone Age!"

Add this to my list of reasons that we're doomed. Whenever you suggest even the slightest movement toward sustainability, the immediate and predictable response is: "You want us to go back to the Stone Age!" As if our only two choices are "continue on our current path" or "go back to the Stone Age." Well, gentle reader, I'm here to report that our current path will lead us precisely back to the Stone Age.

FOOD PROVIDES ENERGY, BUT IT TAKES ENERGY TO MAKE FOOD

It has been estimated that pre-industrial societies expended one unit of energy to provide sixteen units of food energy. For industrial society the ratio is reversed. We currently expend twenty units of energy to provide one unit of food energy. This could possibly be considered to be unsustainable.

This situation was achieved by the intensive use of fossil fuels. Fertilizers synthesized from fossil fuels allow us to ignore cycles of natural fertility. Gasoline processed from fossil fuels allows machinery to replace farmers, and for local farms to be replaced by immense operations located far from population centers. In America, food travels an average of over a thousand miles from farm to kitchen. All of this has allowed agriculture to—

Oh! It's a farmer from Iowa who seems to have something important to share.

"Sorry, I need to jump in here to correct your erroneous conclusions."

Erroneous? I just checked online and confirmed that—

"Yes, the corn I grow—sweet and delicious, especially fresh on the cob—*is* shipped thousands of miles. But I reject the notion that it's not grown locally. It's necessary to enlarge our view and consider the big picture. Imagine the grand sweep of the universe, the immense size of our Milky Way galaxy which is a tiny phenomenon in the unimaginable vastness of space."

I generally agree with looking at things from a larger perspective, but I'm not sure what that has to do with—

"The point is that my corn *is* grown locally—right in our very own little solar system. I urge everyone to support local agriculture by buying only earth-grown corn."

OKAY, BACK TO
WHERE WE LEFT OFF

As I was saying... All of this has allowed agriculture to ignore that long-term agricultural health is based on healthy soil. It has allowed agriculture to destroy the soil structure, deplete organic matter, and kill organisms vital to the health of the soil. As a result, the soil effectively becomes dead—a neutral growing medium to which fertility must be added chemically.

The problem is compounded by the fact that we breed plants and animals for maximum productivity. Plants and animals in the wild balance productivity with qualities like vigor, resiliency, and resistance to attack by diseases and harmful insects. In breeding primarily for increased productivity—in selecting for bigger grains and vegetables, more meat, more milk and eggs—we're selecting against all the other qualities.

The result is plants and animals that are poorly equipped against predation and competition, and are more susceptible to disease. This is exacerbated by crowding large numbers of the same species in unnaturally close contact—which is exactly what we do with the monocropping of plants and the factory farming of animals.

DEEPENING THE ADDICTION

To sustain this system we became addicted to the artificial fertilizers required to replace lost fertility, to the herbicides required to suppress weeds, and to the pesticides and fungicides required to fight pests and diseases. We also became addicted to the antibiotics required to keep factory-farmed animals alive and in some semblance of health.

You may have noticed that factory farms do *not* offer tours to America's schoolchildren so they can learn how beef and other meat products are produced. Because if they did, it would turn America's schoolchildren into vegetarians.

Proponents of the genetic engineering of plants and animals conveniently exclude the fact that genetic engineering only worsens the overall dynamic. Proponents focus only on the (questionable) claim that genetically engineered food products pose no threat to human health. But proponents fail to mention that genetic engineering allows us to deepen the addiction—to create plants and animals that allow us to deplete the soil even faster, to apply agricultural chemicals in higher concentrations, to crowd more animals into bigger factory farms.

Initially, agricultural chemicals are "wonder drugs." The bigger the dose, the bigger the yield. But we quickly become addicted. Abandoning the artificial fertilizers would result in sterile soil barely capable of growing weeks. Abandoning the herbicides and fungicides would result in massive losses of crops. Abandoning the antibiotics would result in the deaths of millions of animals.

So, we're addicted to using the chemicals. But over time the chemicals grow less effective. Over time, the harmful insects and diseases develop immune strains and multiply. The yields decrease. Therefore, new chemicals are needed. Stronger chemicals. More expensive chemicals.

In other words, the friendly salesperson from the big agricultural company is equivalent to the drug dealer hanging around your school, forcing you to keep your habit going by stealing your sister's mandolin.

COULD IT BE POSSIBLE THAT
THIS PARALLELS OUR APPROACH
TO OUR PHYSICAL HEALTH?

The answer to this question, in a heavy Swedish accent, is: *Ya shure!* We compromise our immune system in a variety of ways, such as inadequate exercise, food with poor nutritional content, and chemical pollution.

With our immune systems thus weakened, we become increasingly susceptible to diseases that we overcome with antibiotics. One problem with antibiotics is that they further weaken our immune system—thus making us even more susceptible. Another problem with antibiotics is that over time they grow less effective. Over time, diseases develop immune strains and multiply. Therefore, new antibiotics are needed. Stronger antibiotics. More expensive antibiotics.

In other words, the friendly salesperson from the big pharmaceutical company is *also* equivalent to the drug dealer hanging around your school. But this time, you're forced to keep your habit going by stealing your sister's skateboard.

SUICIDE IS A WAY
TO AVOID DEATH

The process of addiction is a movement toward death, toward self-induced destruction. Another word for this dynamic is *suicide*. Suicide rates are high among alcoholics and drug addicts, who are already committing a kind of slow-motion suicide. It's the view of this author that addiction and suicide are two aspects of the same thing—that suicide is addiction taken to its logical extreme.

This is obvious regarding our addiction to environmental degradation—to the destruction of the biological foundation upon which our lives are dependent. This addiction seems like a kind of suicide because it is.

What leads people to commit suicide? The highest indicators, according to experts, are feelings of hopelessness and meaning-lessness. This is the case whether the perceptions that resulted in those feelings bear any relationship to reality.

The feelings of hopelessness and meaninglessness behind the vast majority of suicides are a result of what experts call "distorted patterns of thinking." The distortion results from identifying the meaning of our life so thoroughly with an ideal that when the connection between the ideal and reality becomes irreparably severed we undergo a crises of meaning. If the crisis is deep enough, we may prefer an end to life rather than a life without the ideal.

A striking example of this was the suicide of Mike Boorda, onetime head of the U.S. Navy, because of a potential scandal concerning whether he had worn inappropriate medals. The scandal would have been minor. Yet in his mind, the potential scandal threatened his role in an organization whose motto is "death before dishonor."

His background gives some sense of why that role was so important. As a result of growing up in a troubled family, he had turned to drinking. He was adrift with no direction in life, until the Navy offered a way out. It "replaced alcohol" he said. The Navy saved his life. It gave him a reason to live, a sense of belonging to a "family" he never had. In Mike Boorda's psyche, a few medals were connected to a role that defined his purpose in life. So when a mistake concerning those medals threatened that role, he couldn't live with it.

In such cases, suicide is the result of addiction—of addiction to an ideal. In such cases, it would be possible to abandon the ideal—to let the ideal die. And by doing so, to embrace a larger perspective on life. But this option is rejected.

To put it another way, suicide is the decision to die rather than to evolve. Suicide only becomes an option if we refuse to die to the part of us that clings to an obsolete ideal. So as strange as it sounds, suicide is a way to avoid death.

A NON-HUMOROUS SUMMARY OF
THIS CHAPTER AND SEGUE TO THE
REMAINDER OF THIS BOOK

Our problem, essentially, is that we're stuck in the midst of a critical evolutionary transition. We're stuck on a faulty misperception. We're addicted to a fatal idea. Ultimately, there are two solutions to an addiction. Either the misperception dies or the addict dies. Those are the only two options. And humanity is not choosing the first option.

CHAPTER 7

THE OPPOSITE
OF LIFE IS NOT
WHAT YOU THINK

In the previous chapter, we explored how recovery from addiction requires a kind of dying, how it requires the death of a misperception that's necessary for life—not only to survive, but to evolve toward a more genuine way of life. But if you think about it—if you look at all aspects of the miraculous phenomenon of life—it's clear that death is an integral aspect of life. Life can't exist without death.

If you wanted me to explain it in more detail, I might begin by taking you out to a romantic dinner while discussing how one aspect of physical death, which science calls *necrobiosis*, consists of the continual death and replacement of individual cells throughout the life of an organism. And how *somatic death*—the death of an entire organism—can be seen as necrobiosis in a larger context. We could consider that as an individual cell gives its life for the life of the larger organism, the collection of cells we call an organism gives its life for the larger collection of organisms we call an ecosystem. And that, in each case, both cell and organism are giving their lives for the very thing that gives them life.

Then back at my place, we might share a bottle of wine while we discuss how all of this applies to—

What's that you say? You'd like to discuss what some people refer to as the "little death"—what the French call *la petite mort*—which is something that many people consider to be an integral aspect of life?

Well, maybe later. For now, I'd like to discuss ways in which death is an integral aspect of life in ways that are more relevant to the topic of this book. Here's an interesting question: If death is an integral aspect of life, then does defying death defy life? Let's find out!

LIFE CAN'T EVOLVE
WITHOUT EXTINCTION

In the evolutionary perspective, the vast majority of earth's lifeforms have gone extinct. Yet not without purpose. Their existence served a role in the overall evolution of life. When they no longer served that evolution, they went extinct. And if they hadn't gone extinct, then subsequent lifeforms couldn't have arisen.

For example, if not for the extinction of the dinosaurs then mammals (like us) would still be tiny mouse-like creatures trying to not get squashed by the dinosaurs. The dinosaurs, of course, served future evolution by becoming the fossil fuels that would eventually power our automobiles. And if we don't quickly evolve past our addiction to fossil fuels, we'll soon be going the way of the dinosaurs.

For millions of years, life consisted only of simple one-celled organisms that essentially didn't die. They reproduced by cloning, by splitting into identical copies of themselves. For millions of years, there was no need to evolve. But the growth of those organisms eventually depleted the available food, resulting in life's first major crisis. This crisis was resolved by the development of photosynthesis, which created oxygen as a by-product. Eventually, the atmosphere became filled with an element that was toxic to lifeforms of the time, which resulted in life's second major crisis.

As a result of both crises, many lifeforms died. But life as whole would have ended if some of them didn't evolve. Or to put it another way, if some of them didn't "die" to their old forms to experiment with new forms.

EVOLVE OR DIE™

Such examples, prominent throughout the history of life on earth, has led this author to develop the principle that life, when faced with critical situations, needs to *Evolve or Die*™—the name of another series of overpriced seminars.

Next series starts soon. Book early to reserve a spot, especially if you missed out on the Meaningful Connection™ *seminar.*

Consider that all forms of life must obey the principles of the dynamic pattern we call an *ecology*. Every form of life has a role in that pattern, and when that role is threatened it results in a crisis. To escape that crisis, the form of life must evolve in a way that successfully adapts itself to a new means to fit into the dynamic and ever-changing pattern. That's the trick. Evolutionary advances are only successful if they result in forms of life that obey the pattern.

THIS ALL APPLIES TO
PSYCHOLOGICAL EVOLUTION

All of us have internalized ideas that form aspects of our self-identities. Eventually, these ideas may prove to be misguided or limited. But getting rid of them isn't an easy or simple matter. We experience them not as *ideas* about ourselves, but *as* ourselves. It could be said (I'll just go ahead and say it) that we've become *addicted* to them.

The ego generally changes in a fundamental way only when it has to, only when living out of its internalized assumptions absolutely doesn't work anymore. The ego has to *really* lose, to comprehend the full depths of the cost. In the context of addiction and recovery, it's the moment of *bottoming out*. It's the realization that what we're clinging to is killing us. In order to get rid of them—to separate ourselves from them—part of us has to die.

Memoirs and literary works are full of accounts of such experiences, described in ways such as "the ground falling away beneath me" or "the world inside me coming apart." In all cases, the old pattern had to die, and the individual had to go through a dying process along with it.

A VALUABLE
PSYCHOLOGICAL STRATEGY

This dying process is closely associated with depression, which we experience as a kind of dying—of feeling internally or psychologically dead. As this author sees it, depression is a result of refusing to let go of something that needs to die.

To be clear, I'm not talking about depression as a result of chemical imbalance or other physical causes. I'm talking about depression that's a result of purely psychological causes. As for this kind of depression, this author has developed a valuable psychological strategy. This strategy has helped this author many times. Perhaps it would help you as well.

Whenever this author experiences the first signs of depression, he asks himself the following: *What has to die? What obsolete goal, self-perception, attitude, or assumption do I need to die to?*

I don't always have the answer. And even if I do, it doesn't substitute for the actual process of dying. But it often points me in the right direction. Perhaps it would for you as well.

WHAT IF WE REFUSE TO DIE?

What if we avoid the psychological deaths that are necessary to more fully live? What kind of life do we have if we refuse to die? In the view of playwright Eric Bentley, all psychological problems are one problem: "the refusal to let go of certain habits, the refusal to die":

Ideally, we should be able to shed habits as a snake sheds its skin. We should be virtuosos in the art of dying. But man is the sick animal, and when we say he doesn't know how to live, we mean he doesn't know how to die. He prefers the life-in-death of severe neurosis.

The life-in-death of severe neurosis—that would be one way to answer the question. There are other words to describe this condition. But whatever we call it, it's not a fun, satisfying, or life-affirming condition. The expression "lives of quiet desperation" comes to mind.

All of this suggests that the dynamic of *evolve or die* also applies to mental life. I found some quotes from a couple of philosophers—really good ones—who express this idea in similar ways. As Søren Kierkegaard put it, "To venture causes anxiety, but not to venture is to lose oneself." Or as Simone de Beauvoir put it, "Life is occupied in both perpetuating itself and in surpassing itself; if all it does is maintain itself, then living is only not dying."

DEATH IS NECESSARY TO LIFE
AS WELL AS TO THE IDEOLOGIES
BY WHICH WE UNDERSTAND LIFE

The fear of death occurs when our worldview is seriously challenged, when we're facing the limitations of any belief in which we've invested our self-image. But going through that death is the only way our understanding can evolve.

B. J. O. Nordfeldt wrote: "To grasp the truth you must first break your idols." By "idols" he meant assumptions or belief systems that limit full understanding. The statement was made regarding art, but it applies to "idols" in any aspect of life.

The evolutionary leap which science calls a *paradigm shift* requires old theories to die in order to make room for new theories. As with evolutionary leaps in life, paradigm shifts in science don't necessarily negate all previous theories. Einstein's physics didn't negate Newton's, but corrected its anomalies by enlarging the perspective—by seeing its truths within a larger and more inclusive truth.

In his *Scientific Autobiography*, physicist Max Planck wrote, "A new scientific truth does not triumph by convincing its opponents and making them see the light, but rather because its opponents eventually die, and a new generation grows up that is familiar with it." If we don't allow obsolete ideas to die within us, they'll die with us.

PERHAPS YOU DON'T
THINK THIS IS RELEVANT
TO OUR SITUATION?

As will become abundantly clear throughout the remainder of this book, the principle of *evolve or die* continues to apply to humanity. But it applies in a new way. Before humanity, obsolete species had to die—species that no longer served productive roles within their ecosystems, species that became evolutionary "dead-ends."

In the evolution of humanity, only obsolete ideas have to die. There's only one basic idea that has to die, but the problem is that we've built every aspect of our civilization on the basis of that one idea. If we don't care to examine it, life will push us into looking— gently at first, and then with increasing urgency. Life wants the idea to go extinct. It will succeed, sooner or later. Life always triumphs in the end. But if we refuse to let go of that one idea, then life is left with little choice over what to do.

TWO SOLUTIONS TO A
NON-EXISTENT PROBLEM

There are abundant reasons to consider death to be an integral and necessary aspect of life. But for some curious reason, a lot of people consider death to be a problem that needs to be solved. Especially, and primarily, the idea that this lovely body we inhabit will someday be food for worms.

But if death is an integral aspect of life, then what happens if we attempt to fix it? This remainder of this chapter will explore humanity's two main ways of trying to fix something that's not broken. We'll begin with the most popular and well-known method. Then we'll move on to the method that's a distant second, but is rapidly increasing in popularity.

THE SOLUTION TO MORTALITY, ACCORDING TO RELIGION

As we've journeyed together on our exploration of why we're doomed, we've often encountered the problem of *greed*. As we previously concluded (by all of us together, but with me doing most of the concluding) greed defies life. Or is opposed to life. Or something like that.

Greed is more than just hogging all the Girl Scout cookies and refusing to share, especially Thin Mints. Many of us have been greedy in this way. But many of us have not. I've shared Thin Mints with many people. Many people have shared Thin Mints with me. Many people have bought me Jell-O shots when they're drunk. Not so much when they're sober, but that's not the point.

We're all greedy, to some degree. And we're all responsible for a civilization that's greedy, to some degree. Do you want to know why we're doomed? Because if you bring up the idea that to survive we need to create a civilization that's not based on greed, the response will be: "But we're not greedy!"

We prefer to think of ourselves as non-greedy because greed is widely considered to be not-nice. We consider ourselves to be nice people who never steal the neighbor's pig. We tend to limit our definition of greed to things we don't do, so we can present ourselves in public as fine upstanding citizens. And because we're fine upstanding citizens perhaps we attend a church, a place where we're reminded of our relationship with the universe and the force which created it and keeps it running smoothly and not freaking out all over.

Religion puts greed near the top of their not-to-do list, along with adultery and coveting the neighbor's pig and some other things I don't remember offhand.

Wait... I think *killing* is one of them.

But religion tends to ignore the types of greed that cause environmental destruction and our addiction to economic growth. And come to think of it, religion doesn't seem to do much about stopping that annoying *killing* thing that keeps happening.

You know, that *war* thing. Because greed has something to do with that, too.

But what can you expect, when so many people subscribe to a version of religion which goes something like, "Believe what the church says and you can live forever for all eternity and it doesn't matter what happens to the world."

Hmm... Eternal life for me and it doesn't matter what happens to the world. That sounds a bit self-centered. It may possibly be construed as a tad *egotistical*, don't you think?

Not *all* religious folks are like this, of course. I know of religious people—and of entire congregations—who are deeply committed to advancing human rights, to ending injustice, to reducing economic disparity, to stopping war, to halting the destruction of "God's Country." Unfortunately, they only make up 2.3 percent of the religious population.

Can you imagine if the number was 100 percent? Hell, I might even join a church. I hear the bingo parties are pretty goddamn fun. I would probably have to stop cussing, though. But I'd be okay with that, as long as I didn't have to believe in a narrow, selfish, anthropocentric version of God.

Does that make me sound judgmental? Is being judgmental one of the "no-no's"?

ONLY ONE SPECIES IS
AFRAID OF DEATH

One aspect of theology, if not the dominant aspect, has been to come up with a number of creative solutions to the "problem" of death. Curiously (and revealingly) we only consider death to be a problem for *human* life. We don't consider it to be a problem for non-human life, which dissolves into the same soil into which we will eventually dissolve. We postulate no heaven beyond earth—no series of karmic rebirths—for the souls of plants and animals.

Except possibly for our pet dog Noodle that will go to "doggy heaven," which may or may not be part of "regular heaven."

Maybe it's sort of like the dog area of a park? Theological literature is curiously silent on the issue.

The tendency for the question to begin and end with humanity reveals the self-centeredness behind it. Death is only a problem for human beings. More specifically, it's only a problem for the human ego, since for those of us who have transcended the ego the problem disappears. We may fear bodily death, but we fear more the death of the separate self. This must be the primary death we fear, because after going through that death we transcend *all* fears. After going through that death, the prospect of the death of the physical body—the "clay garment" worn by life—is no longer a concern.

WHY RELIGION?

The root meaning of the word *religion* is "re-link" or "re-connect." The purpose of religion is to re-establish a connection that broke. What broke was our pre-conscious unity with life. Self-awareness severed our unity with life, and religion arose as a way to re-establish that unity.

Metaphorically speaking, our unity was severed when we left the Garden of Eden. Or rather, when we got kicked out after Eve ate the fruit of self-awareness. (Always blame the woman, eh?) Suddenly, we had the knowledge of good and evil. We also had the knowledge that we were naked, which led to fig leaves becoming humanity's first fashion statement.

We also had the knowledge of ourselves as individual forms of life. For consciousness to become self-reflective, it required an individual self to do the reflecting. And it didn't take long for that individual self to come to a profound realization: *That individual self is going to die.*

For the first time on earth, a form of life became aware of the miracle of being alive. Unfortunately, the awareness of death was interpreted as such a major problem that the miracle of being alive was overshadowed by knowing that experiencing the miracle was only temporary.

A FUNDAMENTAL CHOICE

The emergence of self-reflective consciousness was a dangerous development. According to the book of Genesis, the result was that the earth was "cursed." This is definitely true if we take this to mean not that the earth became bad or evil, but that it was in for a lot of trouble—that is was "cursed" by the appearance of a dangerous development in one of its lifeforms.

According to Genesis, the emergence of self-reflective consciousness brought both positive and negative potentials. Both are included in the Book of Genesis, and are directly related to how we respond to the problem of death. According to Genesis 2:16-17

> And the Lord God commanded the man, saying, Of every tree of the garden thou mayest freely eat: But of the tree of the knowledge of good and evil, thou shalt not eat of it: for in the day that thou eatest thereof thou shalt surely die.

Yet according to Genesis 3:4-5

> And the serpent said unto the woman, Ye shall not surely die: For God doth know that in the day ye eat thereof, then your eyes shall be opened.

Genesis 2:16-17 warns us that self-reflective awareness brings with it the burden of choosing good from evil, along with awareness of physical mortality—the awareness that "thou shalt surely die." This is our "Fall." But Genesis 3:4-5 explains our potential to "Rise"—to expand our awareness, to "open our eyes," to achieve a state in which we "shall not surely die" because we realize that eternity exists within us.

Both potentials had to arrive simultaneously. An evolutionary rise was not possible without first experiencing a fall. Both were a result of the development of an individual self. Our choice is whether we remain stuck on that self or expand that self.

THE PINNACLE OF EVOLUTION?

In the introduction to this book, this author pondered the question of whether humanity is the pinnacle of evolution. This author questioned the claim that we're the pinnacle of evolution because we dominate the earth to produce Chick-n-Minis and Bacon and Cheese Whoppers.

Surely there's something special about humanity. But it's misguided to ask whether humanity is superior to the rest of life. Our only claim to superiority—the only thing that makes us special—is our awareness. If we don't develop that awareness, we destroy any claim to superiority as we degrade the ability of the planet to support life. Only by evolving wisdom—by developing the ability to use that awareness appropriately—are we fully expressing what makes us special. And when we do, the idea of being superior becomes obsolete.

THE EGO CAN BE VERY CLEVER, AND I DON'T MEAN THAT AS A COMPLIMENT

Being stuck on the ego means we're aware that the separate self is going to die. We don't want to die, but we don't want to give up the ego. So what do we do? How can we retain the benefits of the ego yet get rid of that pesky "awareness of mortality" problem that comes with the ego?

This is a very tricky thing to pull off, but the ego is very clever. It's so clever that it doesn't even realize that it did it.

Let's begin with Christianity as our first example, because everyone is familiar with it. Christianity is so pervasive in our culture that even non-Christians are aware of the concepts. Even non-Christians are aware that if two people get together "in the Biblical sense" it means they met to do something other than study the Bible.

If I used another religion, such as Zoroastrianism, hardly anybody would be able to relate. (Zoroastrianism is a real religion, look it up.) Hardly anybody understands the concepts of Zoroastrianism, or is familiar with the trials and tribulations undertaken by the great Zoroaster to establish whatever it is that he established.

I'm not really familiar with Zoroastrianism myself. The only thing I remember offhand is a parable in which Zoroaster performed a miracle by turning water into whiskey. He did it by adding grains and fermenting the mixture. I realize that lots of people do this, but it's still pretty miraculous in my opinion.

So... *Christianity*. A couple thousand years ago there was a carpenter from Nazareth called Jesus. He went into the desert and achieved enlightenment, or nirvana, or samadhi—or whatever term you use to describe unity with all life and existence. He "died" to the skin-encapsulated ego, to the individual person called Jesus, and became "reborn" as Christ. He dwelled in a state of eternity. Or in other words *heaven*. Not a place we go after we die, but a condition of timelessness we achieve after dying to the separate self. And after achieving this state of unity, he became able to most fully love—to love unconditionally, to love without attachment. It could even be said (actually, many people have said it) that he *became* love. And this inclusive sense of love was not only for all people, but for all creation.

The Jesus story is pretty great, eh? Unfortunately, after Jesus died people were free to modify the story without him there to say, "Um, that's not what I said."

I actually have a recording of a conversation that took place the week after Jesus died. The recording was made on an extremely primitive tape recorder. Instead of magnetic tape, it used rope woven from juniper bark. The audio quality isn't great, but it's good enough to make out the following conversation. *(This excerpt was edited from a much longer recording which includes lots of jokes about sheep and numerous songs praising the glory of wheat)*:

THOMAS: "Well, now that Jesus is dead we should probably 'lighten up' his message. It's not incredibly marketable, you know? I mean, that whole thing about *dying to the separate self*... it's so *extreme*."

ADRIAN: "I agree. Also, there's a problem in how his message threatened the powers that be, leading to him being crucified. Having your spiritual leader nailed to a cross isn't exactly the most marketable image."

THOMAS: "Actually, it could be *extremely* marketable. We just need to put a little 'spin' on his message."

And the spin doctors got to work. Eventually, they came up with the following message: Rather than following the example of Jesus by dying to the separate self to become love, keep the ego and love Jesus for doing the dying for us.

Pretty good, eh?

The ego's interpretation of religion makes heaven a state beyond earth rather than a journey while on earth. Rather than uniting heaven and earth, heaven becomes "later" and the earth becomes "it doesn't matter." Rather than live this life to the fullest, the goal is to get this "Vale of Tears" over with because the *real* living is later.

The ego's interpretation of religion substitutes a transcendent being for a transcendent unity with life. It invents a symbol for that unity, then claims unity by worshipping the symbol. By claiming allegiance to the symbol, we're "saved." Rather than a lifelong process of aligning ourselves with that unity, the journey is complete. If we think we've found it, there's no reason to keep looking. "I'll never die" means "I'll never evolve."

Brilliant! Reinforce the ego while claiming to transcend it. As the song says, "Everybody wants to go to heaven, but nobody wants to die."

It's such a great bargain. Only one basic question: "Do you believe?" Say "yes" and you're in. Free pizza for all eternity and your jeans never make your butt look fat. It's the most marketable message in human history.

WOULD YOU LIKE SOME
FREE LITERATURE?

When I say *marketable*, I mean it. I've been handed quite a few pamphlets over the years, trying to convince me to join the club. And prominent in every single one is the assurance that dying is something you can take off your to-do list.

Here's something from a little pamphlet that a nice Asian woman handed me the other day: "God so loved the world that He gave His one and only son, that whoever believes in Him shall not perish, but have eternal life."

And just in case you missed that, it was repeated later as a suggested prayer: "Thank you for forgiving my sins and giving me eternal life." As an aside, that "forgiving of sins" part is pretty great too. Eternal life, plus no more sins as an added bonus. I'd say God deserves more than just a "thank you," don't you? Does God have a tip jar?

Wait... I just checked the pamphlet again, and it's in there *three* times! "The witness is this, that God has given us eternal life."

Wait... *four* times! "You can know on the basis of His promise that Christ lives in you and that you have eternal life from the very moment that you invite Him in."

Apparently, avoiding death is a very good selling point, since they repeat it so often. But shouldn't there be something about affirming life? Could it be that people are drawn to religion less to affirm life than to escape death?

I've done extensive research in this area, and have never found a selling point such as the following. Imagine a nice Asian woman handing you a pamphlet with this message:

Have you been experiencing that "trapped in the separate self" feeling? Do you want to escape the trap? All you have to do is achieve unity with the eternal by expanding your awareness beyond exclusive identification with your time-bound self. Imagine your new life, dedicated not to personal satisfaction, but to loving all existence. Of course, this will be opposed by

powerful forces and you'll probably end up getting crucified.
But it will be for a good cause.

I suspect it wouldn't be really effective. I suspect that if there was a religion based on this message, people would "vote with their feet" by walking away from this religion toward a religion that isn't quite so demanding.

HEY, STOP PICKING ON CHRISTIANITY, YOU BULLY!

If it seems like I'm putting all the blame on Christianity, sorry for the false impression. To be fair to Christianity, many Christians are disturbed by the same distortions of Christianity that disturb me. And those distortions are in no way unique to Christianity. I'm not anti-Christian. In fact, some of my best Christian friends are Christian.

But it's probably too late for diplomacy. If any Christians read what wrote in this chapter, they probably revile me.

Here's the point I want to make: I'm not picking on Christianity. I'm picking on the ego. Because the ego has screwed up (and will screw up) any religion it gets its hands on. Christ didn't come up with the idea of The Crusades. That was the ego's brilliant idea. Look at how some extremist egos get a hold of the Muslim religion and become suicide-bombing fundamentalists who declare Fatwas and murder people who make fun of them.

Just for the record, I'm not making fun of them.

The ego has screwed up the core message of Zoroastrianism, whatever it is. The ego is currently screwing up The Church of the Silent Monkey. The religion has only been in existence since I made it up just now, but already the core message is becoming distorted. The original tenet of "Treat people as you wish to be treated" has been turned into "If you don't get caught, then it's okay."

Contrasted with mainstream religion is the New Age movement. Those affluent "spiritual but not religious" folks are *so* evolved. They realize that most of what's in the Bible should be understood as metaphor. They understand that heaven and hell are states of mind, and that all the rituals and the *thou-shall-this* and *thou-shall-that* business was appropriate for a "less evolved" level of human consciousness.

Yet as the worst of mainstream religion ignores this world for the next, the worst of the New Age movement ignores this world for the quest for personal enlightenment. There's not much time left over for the world with all the channeling of past lives, lucid dreaming, tapping into crystal energy, releasing the chakras (or is it *awakening* the chakras?) and using positive visualization to "create my own reality."

Speaking of *creating your own reality*... As I understand it, the idea is to create a visualization of what you want, which interacts with existence to alter reality just for you.

Hmm... Altering reality just for you. That sounds a bit self-centered. It may possibly be construed as a tad *egotistical*, don't you think?

It sounds to me like a variation of the idea of praying to the creator of the universe for what you want, which interacts with existence to alter reality just for you. The New Age version sounds like the same thing, except it leaves out God as the middleman. I guess that's a little less egotistical since it doesn't bother God, who's possibly busy with things more important than altering reality just for you.

MANIFESTING $$$

If Christianity believes that matter and spirit are separate, the New Age movement affirms they're united. Yet it often uses this to justify material affluence as a sign of spiritual progress. Have you ever heard of the expression *manifesting abundance?* I suppose it's important to manifest a lot of abundance. I mean, those retreats in Sedona aren't free.

Brilliant! Reinforce the ego while claiming to transcend it. As the song says, "Everybody wants to achieve samadhi, but nobody wants to die to the separate self."

To be fair, many New Age adherents are also concerned about issues such as environmental protection and social justice. Again,

I'm not faulting the movement itself. As with any religion and/or belief system, I'm faulting the egotistical interpretations of it.

But I imagine that, once again, it's too late for diplomacy. Now I've assured myself of being reviled by the New Age community.

Who else can I convince to revile me? I'm probably already reviled by the atheist community for taking religion seriously. At this rate, I'm going to end up reviled by everybody. But I don't mind. Being reviled is a dirty job, but somebody's got to do it.

HUMOR!

This chapter hasn't contained much fun. So let's end the religion section of this chapter with a religious joke:

> *Jesus finally returned after 2,000 years, and he was sure hungry! So he went to a café. After downing an order of scrambled eggs and hash browns, he told the waitress to prepare for his Second Helping.*

Hopefully the rest of this chapter will be more fun. Because it's not just religion that's trying to solve the problem of mortality. It's also science! Can you believe it? Two opposite ways of trying to fix something that's not broken.

THE SOLUTION TO MORTALITY, ACCORDING TO SCIENCE

The previous sections of this chapter explored the views of our friend *Dogmatic Religious Person*, who personifies the superficial and ego-based interpretation of religion. Now, it's time to explore the views of another friend, *Dogmatic Materialist* (sometimes known as *Dogmatic Atheist* or *Dogmatic Anti-Religious Person*). If the previous sections of this chapter were about what the ego does to religion, then the remaining sections of this chapter are about what the ego does to science.

It's important to recognize that scientists are people, too. They laugh and love and get into dysfunctional relationships, just like the rest of us. They think the bartender is flirting with them even though the bartender is just being friendly, just like the rest of us.

Just for the record, I never do that thing with the bartender—confusing friendly service for romantic interest. What I mean is that I hardly ever do it. What I mean is that I only do it when I'm in a bar.

Scientists are also subject to faulty starting principles, just like the rest of us. For example, they disregard anything that can't be measured. They call this *objectivity*, which means to remove subjective bias by disregarding anything that can't be quantified. But leaving out subjectivity leaves out some things that maybe shouldn't be left out. Such as life and consciousness.

Many of us believe that life and consciousness exist, based on the criteria of being alive and experiencing consciousness. But science—at least the kind of science practiced by our friend *Dogmatic Materialist*—tells us, "You're being superstitious and immature and if you don't stop it I won't play with you anymore and I won't let you borrow my basketball." Although they say this in a more mature way and don't mention the basketball.

What about a *soul?* Do we have one of those? We can probably guess how our friend *Dogmatic Materialist* would reply. But let's ask anyway, just for fun.

What do you think, Dogmatic Materialist? Do we have a soul?

"Of course not. We can't have a soul because that's immaterial, and only material things exist."

Why do we believe we have a soul?

"Sorry, but you're being fooled."

By who?

"What do you mean?"

If I'm being fooled, then who—or what—is doing the fooling?

"It's merely consciousness. You're being fooled by consciousness into making you think you have a soul."

But according to the materialistic science you advocate so dogmatically, consciousness is an illusion. Mental activity—including consciousness—is nothing more than material reactions.

"Well in that case, matter is fooling you. Matter is fooling you with the consciousness you don't have into believing you have a soul which doesn't exist."

Thanks for clearing that up, Dogmatic Materialist!

FAULTY STARTING PRINCIPLES
LEAD TO FAULTY CONCLUSIONS

When operating with faulty starting principles, efforts to explain things take bizarre turns. Let's consider the evolution of humanity. What's the primary factor in human evolution? Obviously it has to do with the evolution of consciousness, right? I mean, if we examine the evolution of *Homo sapiens*, the physical form of our bodies has barely changed in the past million years. The biggest change was in consciousness. And if we examine our current level of "evolution" (I'm trying not to laugh) compared to the few wise and compassionate individuals that have achieved something like what it means to be fully human, that's purely a change in consciousness.

We can definitely say that our tools have evolved. We have physical evidence of this, such as comparing the horrible cathode ray tube television sets from the 1950s to the high-definition flat panel digital televisions of today.

That type of physical evidence is the only type of proof accepted by "certain scientists" (you know who you are). According to those scientists, human evolution is nothing more than the evolution of technology. Human evolution can be reduced to the brilliant segue in Stanley Kubrick's *2001 Space Odyssey*, where one of the proto-human apes tosses a bone—the first tool—into the air, and it becomes a spaceship. (This brilliant jump cut condenses millions of years of evolution into a few seconds, thus preventing the long movie from being even longer.)

Thus, evolution is reduced to what has been called *technological evolution*. This idea of evolution holds that—with humanity—evolution has become "directable" or "purposeful."

There are a few faulty assumptions associated with this idea. It assumes that evolution had no "direction" or "purpose" before us. And it assumes that we've been "freed" from the rest of life, and that our freedom from the rest of life means that we have no responsibility toward the rest of life. Therefore, life can't be worthy of ethical consideration. We can do anything we want. The earth doesn't matter.

Hey, wait a minute... *Dogmatic Materialist* says the earth doesn't matter? Isn't that the same thing that *Dogmatic Religious Person* says?

YES IT IS!

Although science is supposedly the opposite of religion, the fundamentalist versions of both science and religion come to the conclusion that we bear no responsibility to earthly existence. This is inevitable when we put the ego in charge.

BETTER LIVING THROUGH GENETIC ENGINEERING

Technological evolution is devoted to advancing the interests of the human ego at the expense of the rest of existence. This is most obvious in genetic engineering. We have the key to the internal "map" of life, and can alter it to suit our own designs. We can literally engineer life. One book on the subject declares optimistically that genetic engineering "will eventually enable us to turn the workings of all living things on earth—the entire biosphere—to the particular advantage of our own species."

Hmm... Turn the workings of all living things on earth to the particular advantage of our own species. That sounds a bit self-centered. It may possibly be construed as a tad *egotistical*, don't you think?

With genetic engineering, evolution is no longer "trapped" in the gradual and "purposeless" movement of before, but can be sped up and directed in ways we choose. The "speeding up" of life is seen as a good thing by futurist Peter Russell, because "the rapid acceleration so characteristic of today is heading us toward an evolutionary leap."

In the opinion of this author, a *genuine* evolutionary leap will only happen when we give up such ideas, when we realize the hubris of trying to dominate life.

I, ROBOT?

An excellent example of the assumptions behind technological evolution can be found in an article by Marvin Minsky, entitled "Will Robots Inherit the Earth?" According to Minsky, after we "imagine ways in which novel replacements for worn body parts might solve our problems of failing health," we can "invent strategies to augment our brains and gain greater wisdom."

Such a view is based on the assumption that wisdom is something that must be added to the brain, rather than something achieved by subtracting what blocks its full expression—by evolving beyond the ego, by becoming more conscious.

Of course, you won't be receptive to such an idea if you don't believe that consciousness is real—if you're a dogmatic materialist like Marvin Minsky who, in the course of his article, feels compelled to address the alleged existence of the "vital ingredient" or "missing essence" referred to as "sentience, consciousness, spirit or soul":

> Philosophers write entire books to prove that because of this deficiency, machines can never feel or understand the kinds of things that people do. Yet every proof in each of these books is flawed by assuming, in one way or another, what it purports to prove—the existence of some magical spark that has no detectable properties. I have no patience with such arguments.

If consciousness is solely a product of discrete thoughts—a digital process of organizing bits of data—then it's reasonable to believe that it can be contained within computers. After replacing our bodies with machines, we can use nanotechnology to replace our brains. "Once delivered from the limitations of biology," writes Minsky, "we will decide the length of our lives—with the option of immortality."

With human engineering, we would have the opportunity to literally reinvent not only ourselves, but also our descendants. Minsky concludes his article "Will Robots Inherit the Earth?" by answering, "Yes, but they will be our children."

THE ENDGAME OF
TECHNOLOGICAL EVOLUTION

Thus, humanity becomes electronic minds in mechanical bodies. The perceived "limitations of biology" have been solved by abandoning biology. Therefore, mortality has been eliminated. But only by eliminating life. Our non-biological replacements won't die, but only because they aren't alive in the first place.

Only a form of life can be alive. And as a robot can't be alive, neither can a computer be conscious. Computers will never achieve the real thing, although they're getting much better at mimicking it. There are already computers that can fool us into thinking they're conscious. But if we think a computer can be truly conscious, we're only fooling ourselves.

THE FINAL FRONTIER?

Another distorted form of technological evolution involves the exploration of space. Rather than evolve in a way that deepens our relationship to life on earth, technological evolution leads us away from the earth. Space exploration can be seen as the attempt to transcend the limits of space and time. But not by transcending the ego. It retains the ego, which is what keeps us trapped in space and time. It searches for new earths—new

"Edens"—on which to start over. It seeks to spread our partial awareness to other planets after we've destroyed our own.

Hmm... That gives me an idea. That scenario could make a great movie. It could be turned into a major motion picture, coming soon to a theater near you. It could be called *A NEW EDEN*. Here's a plot summary:

> *A small party of people leave an increasingly toxic and war-torn earth to start over on another planet. But they unknowingly bring with them the same assumptions that led to earth's downfall. One of the people opens a McDonalds. Another demands to be called the "banker" and creates debt-based money to begin an economic system based on unlimited growth. One of the people discovers oil, and another person shoots that person and takes the oil. One of the people starts an un-sustainable agriculture system and hires a couple other people to do the work for sub-minimum wage.*
>
> *Soon they exhaust the resources of the new planet and the economy collapses. Nobody can afford Big Macs and the people begin dying of starvation. The last two survivors have a conversation. One proposes that the entire mission was doomed from the start, and that they need to embark upon a new mission: return to earth and convince what's left of humanity to adopt principles based on living in harmony with life. (An earlier scene established this character as an unrealistic dreamer.)*
>
> *In an extremely emotional scene, the idealistic dreamer person dies. This makes the last person sad because it means there's nobody to have sex with.*
>
> *The last person goes back to earth to put together a new crew. Then they leave to find a new planet. Thus, the stage is set for the sequel: ANOTHER NEW EDEN.*

The movie includes a romantic subplot, of course, which means some softcore space sex. The movie gives audiences what they want, which is hope. And softcore space sex.

TWO NON-SOLUTIONS,
AND THE REAL SOLUTION

By avoiding the same thing that religion is avoiding, science took the opposite path to arrive at the same place. In both cases, the ego is triumphant. By attempting to solve a non-existent problem, both paths miss the real answer. It's a simple answer, really. Just accept that we're going to die, and make the most of this one life we have. Why do so many people have a problem with that answer?

CHAPTER 8

IF EVERYBODY IS AGAINST WAR, THEN WHY DOES IT KEEP HAPPENING?

This is basically a humor book, with some philosophy in between the jokes. But how I can I make jokes about something as serious as war? I mean, things like destroying the ability of the planet to support life and basing our economy on a doomed pyramid scheme heading toward collapse are naturally funny. But war is a whole other thing.

I'm reminded of a memory from one of our Iraq wars (I can't remember which one, I get our wars all mixed up). It was near the end of the war, when our military was killing tens of thousands of retreating solders in what was being described as a "turkey shoot." And on the news, an evangelist was shouting to a crowd of true believers "This is proof that God is on our side!" to which the crowd roared its approval. There are a lot of things I could say about this, but none of them are humorous.

Here's an idea: What if I respond in the form of a limerick? Limericks are fun, right? Here's the perspective of one of those "true believers" expressed as a limerick:

Praise the Lord and Pass the Ammunition

Please ask not for whom tolls the bell
Because killing for Jesus is swell
The Iraqis weren't "saved"
So morality's waived
They were just going to end up in hell

This is a good idea. I was wondering how to make the subject of war less... oh, I don't know... less *sad* or something. I think limericks will work.

By the way, *Praise the Lord and Pass the Ammunition* is the title of an American patriotic song written in 1942 in response to the attack on Pearl Harbor, and was a popular expression throughout World War II.

THE ROOTS OF WAR

As for human activities that are destructive of life, war is high on the list. Imagine how many plants and animals have suffered because of war. Every mortar shell knocks leaves from trees and makes worms really nervous. Every time a torpedo sinks a ship, countless fish are annoyed. Every time a city goes up in smoke and flames, flocks of birds have coughing fits.

War also kills people.

Since war is generally thought of as not good, how about if we get to the roots of it so that we can stop doing it? I mean, if we're going to get to the roots of something, why not make it something worthwhile? By comparison, trying to get to the roots of something like *poor interior decorating choices* just doesn't have the same... is *appeal* the right word?

Okay, here we go. The roots of war. I've got my research materials in front of me. I've also got a bottle of beer in front of me. It's one of my favorites, a Deschutes Black Butte Porter. As the saying goes: *Better to have a bottle in front of me than a frontal lobotomy.*

THE WAR WITHIN

As for the roots of war, let's put the question to the members of the human race that we consider to be wise or enlightened. *(Hmm... Are these the members of the human race who've "won" the race?)* When asked about the roots of war, the universal answer is something about "the war within."

Where in heck did I put my beer?

To correctly interpret the meaning of *the war within*, it's important to rid ourselves from interpretations by non-wise and non-enlightened members of the human race. In other words, interpretations by the assorted New Age gurus telling us that we can end war by sending out peaceful energy. Sending out peaceful energy probably doesn't hurt. But I'm pretty sure there have been no instances of peaceful energy coursing through a battlefield and inspiring both sides to lay down their weapons and get together for a group hug.

I have something about this in my research materials. Doesn't that sound impressive?—*my research materials*. It makes me sound like a serious writer. I could make it sound even more impressive. I could say something like, *my research materials from my files*. Even though my "files" consists of a shoebox filled with scraps of paper with movie recommendations from people in bars, funny things I heard people say in bars, and things I picked up from websites and magazines while wishing I was in a bar. Not that I have a drinking problem.

Oh, there's my beer.

As for the relevant information from my research materials, I have a quotation by the inspirational author Deepak Chopra, one in a long line who has become very wealthy by marketing watered-down spirituality to affluent yuppies. How else do you think these people sell tons of books? It's sure not by encouraging people to examine the effects of their affluence on earthly life.

Here's what Deepak Chopra wrote about war, in an article about his reaction to the 9/11 attacks: "There can be no safety until the root cause is faced." *Well, I'm glad to know that Deepak and I are "on the same page" as they say. Tell us please, Mr. Chopra, what's the root cause? Does it have something to do with economic imperialism? Is it somehow related to our destructive relationship with the planet?*

Here's our guru's explanation of the root cause: "If you and I are having a single thought of violence or hatred against anyone in the world at this moment, we are contributing to the wounding of the world."

Well, thanks for clearing that up, Dee—*is it all right if I call you Dee?* So if I just have warm, fuzzy feelings for everyone and go shopping, then it's not my fault? *Cool!*

LET'S GET A LITTLE MORE
PRACTICAL, SHALL WE?

To get the ball rolling in a more productive manner, let's bring in something by Michael Ventura, one of the most insightful and fearless writers in this country and hardly anybody has heard of him. *Could it be that's because he goes for the truth and avoids easy "feel good" messages?*

In his essay "What is War?" he begins by noting how he often hears people go down a familiar litany of explanations. He notes that war has been blamed on the struggle for markets and resources, class conflict, patriarchy, fundamentalism, and nationalism.

All of these are undoubtedly factors in war but not the *roots* of war, since, as Ventura continues,

> There were wars long before there were nations, classes and markets; people of the same religion and politics have often battled; to blame the mass behavior on only half the population (male) is to ignore the totality of war. In every war I know about, women have ranted as gung-ho as the men once the action started, and for as long as their side won.

Go Michael! With only 65 words you've debunked a heck of a lot of theories!

WHAT CAUSES THE CAUSES?

I propose that the familiar litany of explanations aren't *wrong,* just *incomplete.* They're contributing causes but not *the* cause. They're branches on the tree, but not the roots.

Perhaps by looking deeper we might come to see how they all fit together. Perhaps acknowledging that war has a variety of contributing causes will end our ideological warfare over which one is the root cause. If so, then what's the next step? What's common to all the factors?

The answer is obvious, isn't it?

Let's analyze the contributing causes and see what they have in common. When you see the answer you'll probably slap yourself on the forehead and exclaim, "Ow! That hurts!"

As for those contributing causes, what they all have in common is *greed*:

- The struggle for markets and resources: We want more stuff than everybody else = *material greed*

- *Class conflict:* My side wants more money than your side = *economic greed*

- *Fundamentalism:* Our ideas about existence are better than everybody else's = *ideological greed*

- *Nationalism:* Our chunk of land unified by a common political system is better than your chunk of land unified by a common political system = *patriotic greed*

- *Patriarchy:* Men can't have babies, but while women are having babies men can organize society in a way that benefits men = *men are greedy jerks*

Whether over resources, money, religious ideologies, or ways to organize society, war is a battle for supremacy. *Greed leads to war.* But we generally fail to acknowledge the connection. This helps explain why—despite the fact that everybody claims to be against war—it keeps happening anyway. We may claim to be against war, but we aren't against greed. And we can't eliminate the effect while retaining the cause.

FUNDAMENTALISM

We commonly think of fundamentalism only in respect to religion. But there are fundamentalists in every area of human endeavor, and the same principles apply to them all. There are fundamentalists aligned with political ideologies, economic ideas, psychological concepts, and types of beer. For example, there are IPA fundamentalists who refuse to acknowledge that the only advantage to IPAs is that they get you drunk faster because you have the chug them quickly before the taste catches up with you.

Let's take a moment to explore political fundamentalism. Individuals on the far extremes of the political spectrum expound views diametrically opposed to each other. To defend those views, each side is forced to deny the faults and weaknesses of its own side, and to deny the strengths and advantages of the other side. Anyone who proudly states their belief in one side or the other is proudly stating, "I'm in denial of half of political reality." Of course, denying half of political reality means that your views will be wrong half the time. But if you're a fundamentalist, are you going to admit this? Probably not.

When a fundamentalist ideology isn't working, it can't be because the fundamentalism is limited. If we attempt to fit life into a partial and limited view, then we need to deny evidence that the ideology is partial and limited. We need to ideologically "kill" the evidence. As a result, to the extent we're personally attached to that partial and limited view we're impelled toward violence in order to defend it. Intellectual violence leads to verbal violence. In extreme cases it leads to physical violence—to tangible attacks against whatever threatens the ideology.

The classic example is the owner of a quarry whose workers discovered primitive human skulls and skeleton fragments. The owner was a fundamentalist Christian—an unquestioning believer in the biblical creation story who detested Darwin's theory of evolution. The discovery presented him with a discrepancy between the ideas in his mind and the evidence before his eyes—a discrepancy he dealt with not by re-examining his ideas but by destroying the evidence.

TERRORISM IS BAD

For those who fear life's ambiguities, fundamentalism brings the promise of absolute certainty. And the allure of that certainty becomes especially powerful concerning religion, when that certainty includes the promise of eternal life.

The fear of ambiguity also fuels terrorism. Psychologist Robert Jay Lifton studied a variety of extremists and terrorists, and concluded that fanaticism breeds on social upheavals that leave people feeling dislocated, that leave them believe their world is falling apart. A strong sense of personal hopelessness combines with an ideology containing an apocalyptic vision that divides the world into good and evil—a vision in which the terrorist is firmly on the side of good. It's a way to end one of life's most troublesome forms of ambiguity in a dangerously simplistic way.

Rather than the line between good and evil passing through us all, the line now lies between *us and them*. From the point of view of a terrorist, they aren't killing people. They're eliminating evil from the face of the earth. They're saving the world. And because they're certain of eternal life in the next world, they have nothing to lose by sacrificing their life in this world. Therefore fundamentalism, taken to its extreme, becomes terrorism— which not only defends its ideology with violence, but advances it with violence.

This absolutely applies to beer fundamentalists such as the IPA terrorists, who are attempting to eliminate all non-IPA options from the tap lists of earth. I shall oppose them at the risk of sacrificing my life. Not to achieve heaven beyond earth, but to avoid the hell on earth of drinking only IPAs.

WE'RE ALL TERRORISTS
SOMETIMES

Few of us fall into such extreme forms of terrorism. But none of us are free of it. We're terrorists every time we say "This is how it is" instead of "This is how I see it." To state a point of view as truth is to deny the validity of all other points of view. It forces others into a dilemma in which the only way they can state their point of view is to violate your truth. It's a declaration of war. It gives others the choice of giving up or becoming equally dogmatic, of surrendering or fighting back.

A GREEDY SPECIES?

Greed is generally considered as a bad thing on a personal one-on-one basis. What happens when two people are acting toward each other based on greed? The smiles become strained. Antagonism rises. Each side begins searching for excuses to hate the other side, to dehumanize them. Tension builds. Eventually, they're fighting.

It's the same thing that happens between nations. The only difference is that nations are throwing bombs at each other, and the two people are throwing...

Oh, they're also throwing bombs. Never mind.

Here's the big question that not many people ask: Could this be happening with humanity as a whole? Is the entire human race at war against something? Is humanity a greedy species?

Well, let's see... We *are* steadily degrading the integrity of every ecosystem on earth, creating mass extinctions of other species, and using more natural resources than the planet can replenish. Humanity is currently using 40 percent of the planet's photosynthetic productivity, or net primary production. Imagine: One species out of earth's millions of species is claiming 40 percent of the earth's production for itself. I guess we *are* a greedy species.

SOME OF US ARE
GREEDIER THAN OTHERS

But the rewards of that greed aren't being distributed equally. Most of that unsustainable affluence is being channeled to only a minority of humanity. How awful! And what nation is the worst in this respect? Here's a clue. In a 1948 State Department Policy Planning Staff Paper, George F. Kennan wrote:

> We have about 50 percent of the world's wealth, but only 6.3 percent of its population. Our real task in the coming period is to devise a pattern of relationships which will permit us to maintain this position of disparity.

Maintain our position of disparity we did! And how! Our success in maintaining our position of disparity was largely responsible for our legendary and awe-inspiring post-war economic boom. As a result, America is number one! Not in education or health care or literacy or happiness. *But we're number one in consumerism!* And by an amazing non-coincidence, we're number one in war. Our military budget is larger than the combined military budgets of the next nine countries in the world. We have 800 military bases worldwide, and we've been at war for 93 percent of our country's history.

Rather than comment in a boring, drawn-out, factual manner on the relationship between unsustainable affluence and war, here's a limerick:

I ♥ Consumerism

There are some things I don't like about war
The reports about death are a bore
As the bullets are popping
I'd rather be shopping
And if we win I can buy so much more

A QUICK DETOUR WHILE
WE'RE ON THE SUBJECT

There's a very interesting tangent related to one of the ways that America maintained its position of disparity. Exploring this in depth would be outside of the parameters of this book envisioned by the author before writing this book destroyed his mind. It has to do with something you might have heard of, about how America sells debt to other countries.

Huh?

Yes, when I first heard that it sounded pretty weird to me, too. Yet curiously, it seems like most people just accept it without exploring what the hell it means.

For those who are interested in this fascinating topic, which will likely help in turning your feelings about America from ☺ to ☹, feel free to conduct research on your own. Do an internet search on topics such as *Bretton Woods Conference* and *Global Reserve Currency.*

You will be fascinated by the discovery that America retained its position of disparity not by being smarter or more industrious than other countries, but by creating blatantly unfair economic arrangements and imposing them on the rest of the world. And you might find it interesting to know that one use of America's outrageously huge military has been to defend those blatantly unfair economic arrangements. Which is another thing you can research on your own.

WHAT IS WAR?

This author is going to boldly declare a new definition of the term. The dictionary definition of war is "open and declared armed fighting." But as I see it, war is something that's not necessarily declared. And it's much more than a bunch of guys (and gals, too—I don't want to discriminate) shooting each other and lobbing heavy exploding things into each other's backyards.

Here's my proposed redefinition: *War is coordinated action with the intent of destroying the integrity of an individual or collective form of life for the unequal gain of another.*

By this definition, a whole lot of activities could be considered to be forms of war. It would mean *colonialism* is war, whether military or economic colonialism. It would mean that *genocide* is a form of war, whether the genocide is overt or subtle—whether the violence is in the form of a direct attack (killing them) or an indirect attack (killing their food supply).

It would also mean—I can hardly consider the thought—that our relationship with all earthly life is a form of war. It would mean that humanity is at war against life. And that this war underlies and leads to wars of nation against nation. Because if everyone was satisfied with what life sustainably provided, then we wouldn't have to wage wars against other nations to get more.

Wars aren't "accidents" for the same reasons that extinct species, clearcut forests, nuclear waste, pollution, and global warming aren't "accidents." War is an inevitable result of our lifestyle.

ARE WE THERE YET?

Are we done now? The answer is "greed causes war," and we can stop there?

No, gentle reader. This author wants to take you *all the way to the roots*. If greed is the cause, then what causes the cause? Is humanity intrinsically greedy? Do we come out of the womb pre-programmed as greedy little devils just itching to grow up and take someone else's stuff? Or are we caring little angels until *[insert your theory here]* diverts us from our genuine nature and knocks us onto the road to greed?

To find out, we're going to make a brief detour to re-visit the fascinating topic of the evolution of human consciousness and its effects on human civilization.

Oooh! Are you as excited as I am?

THE RELATIONSHIP BETWEEN
WAR AND THE EVOLUTION
OF HUMAN CONSCIOUSNESS

The big event in the story happened around 6,000 years ago, when humanity's most serious problem began. When we search for the roots of greed, we're led invariably to the emergence of the ego. Greed didn't exist when individuals were incapable of conceptually separating themselves from each other or their environment. As a result, war as we know it didn't exist.

The pinnacle of Neolithic culture was achieved in the week prior to 6,000 years ago, in the warm, comfy Mediterranean, where there had evolved a complex society that was so ideal that perhaps it was what we refer to as *Eden*. It wasn't perfect (nothing is perfect) but it was a much more peaceful and egalitarian society than what would follow.

Archeological study suggests that their religion was an earth-based spirituality. "They were a bunch of pagans!" you say disapprovingly. "They were a bunch of freaking hippies!" Maybe so, but even if you're not crazy about the "hippie lifestyle" I'm pretty sure you'd prefer it to what came next.

The ego—accompanied by self-reflective consciousness—emerged initially in northern Europe. Why there? I speculate that it had something to do with the rotten weather. It's not hard to imagine. Picture a couple guys harvesting roots in a muddy field. Rain is mixed with light snow. One of the guys lost his blanket. He's cold, damp, and miserable. I imagine his grumpiness building until he eventually shouts, "I am *freezing!*"

And the guy is shocked. He's says to himself, "I just said *I.* That's new, that was never said before. It's an entirely new concept."

Then the other guy asks him, "Hey, what's all this about *I?*"

And the first guy replies, "This is really weird, but *I* said it. Not *you,* but *me. You're* somebody else. *You're* a different person than *me.*"

"I am?" says the other guy.

"Yes you are. You're different from me. And you have a blanket. Hey, gimme your blanket!"

"No!" replies the other guy. "This is *my* blanket! It belongs to *me!*"

Which is when the first guy hits him in the head with a rock and takes his blanket.

And the rest, as they say, is history.

HISTORY!

The historic transition likely began in what is now Scandinavia, famed for originating the concept of *rape and pillage.* I don't think I'm exaggerating when I say that the hippies weren't prepared for what was coming. The transition initiated a succession of ruthless leaders whose main hobby consisted of conquering and killing hippies.

The Age of Earth-Worshipping Hippies came to an end as a result of *The Age of Bloodthirsty Murderers.* Physical conquest coincided with religious conquest. This era marked the historical shift from the worship of the earth to the worship of vengeful male Gods of the sky. A hierarchy developed with God on top, then men, then women—with nature on the bottom.

The hippies weren't crazy about this new religion, but the conquerors were successful in converting most of them with a convincing argument consisting of "Accept this new religion or we'll kill you."

HISTORY = HIS STORY

Did I mention that it was basically *men* doing all this? But to blame war solely on men is misleading. Feminist scholars enthusiastically cite the archaeological evidence of Neolithic settlements in places such as Minoan Crete and Catal Huyuk in present-day Turkey, which suggest that these matriarchal cultures were not only peaceful but also well-planned, prosperous, and egalitarian. But feminist scholars are less enthusiastic about citing the evidence that such societies performed human sacrifice.

Oops!

What's missing from consideration is the evolution of consciousness. Taking this into consideration allows us to answer the troubling question of how a supposedly egalitarian culture could accept the sacrifice of individual citizens. The answer is that before self-reflective consciousness there was no such a thing as an individual citizen because there was no such a thing as an individual.

This might be part of the explanation of why such cultures were egalitarian. Not because of any conscious decision toward equality, but because nobody was able to see themselves as *not* equal. They lived in relative harmony not based on consciously choosing unity, but on the inability to choose otherwise.

Such societies weren't *entirely* peaceful, according to recent research that feminist scholars are also not enthusiastic about. But declaring war—in the way we now envision it—wouldn't have been conceivable at that stage of human consciousness.

My point is that the problem isn't *men* so much as *the ego*. It's just that men developed egos first, or developed them more strongly. Or perhaps it's just that those egos were contained in bigger bodies that could hit harder.

HISTORY, CONTINUED

Although the Scandinavians have now abandoned their war-like ways, at the time they inspired countless imitators. Those imitators introduced many new twists on the original idea. As a result, *The Age of Bloodthirsty Murderers* evolved into *The Age of Empire*.

Nations with arbitrarily designated boundaries attempted to expand those boundaries, to conquer territory for wealth and power. As the East had Egypt under the Pharaohs and the Mongols under Genghis Kahn, the West had the Romans under Caesar and the French under Napoleon. Human history became dominated by a series of empires conquering and expanding until they inevitably overextended themselves and broke up, their boundaries dissolving and their territories becoming enclosed within other boundaries that continued the same process.

That process created a series of ravaged ecosystems in its wake, and turned the fabled Fertile Crescent of the Mediterranean into the degraded environment that it is today.

The Old World of Europe expanded to conquer and colonize the New World of the Americas, pushing farther around the world in search of access to resources—especially to gold. As a result, *The Age of Empire* evolved into *The Age of Imperialism*. Cortez decimated the Aztec culture, as Pizarro did with the Incas. The conquering forces established mines and stripped local vegetation to fuel the smelters. Missionaries tagged along to give the appearance of transcendent purpose, which consisted of "saving" the savages by converting them to the religion of their conquerors.

Imperialism eventually became less overt. Various forms of internal interference could lead to economic concessions or trade imbalances that gave control over a territory without the need for direct military conquest. Civil wars were started in Africa, pitting tribe against tribe to gain access to slaves. The Dutch used opium to disrupt Indonesian society and take over foreign policy, as Britain did with India and China. As such arrangements became formalized, *The Age of Imperialism* evolved into *The Age of Colonialism*.

MANIFEST DESTINY

England formed colonies in North America, which rebelled to form a nation called the United States—a nation that quickly began its own expansion. This expansion was called *Manifest Destiny*. The violence incurred by this expansion was justified by the belief that it was the destiny of the United States to expand its territory over the whole of North America, and to extend its political and economic influences even farther. It was considered to be our historic mission based on the self-declared superiority of ourselves and of our ideas.

Expansion occurred along an edge we called *the frontier*—a boundary between civilization and savagery, order and chaos, law and lawlessness. That edge disappeared when the frontier reached the Pacific Ocean. At this point, the edge began to move outward.

Ironically, the United States—which was founded as a rebellion against colonialism and imperialism—became a late player in the same game. Manifest Destiny became the *Monroe Doctrine*, which held that the United States had the right to advance its own interests throughout the entire Western Hemisphere.

The United States took over Hawaii and Samoa, and went to war with Spain to acquire the Philippines, Guam, and Puerto Rico. But by the late 1800's there wasn't much territory left for easy conquest, and public opinion was moving against blatant forms of colonialism.

So colonialism became economic, which was achieved by enslaving other countries by means of financial agreements putting them at a perpetual disadvantage. One method of doing this was to extend loans for Western-style development that trapped countries into destroying their environments to pay steadily-compounding interest on loans that could never realistically be paid off.

MORE LIMERICKS!

Here's a limerick about trapping countries into destroying their environments to pay steadily-compounding interest on loans that can never realistically be paid off:

I ♥ *Economic Colonialism*

It's great to indebt other nations
For exploitive financial relations
You say rainforests fell
To pay loans?—Oh do tell!
Let's forget it and drink some libations

Here's a limerick about Manifest Destiny:

I ♥ *Manifest Destiny*

It's so cool to create a new nation
Let's exploit it—I mean, who likes to ration?
Just push out the Apache
And with nature get nasty
Then we'll pave it and take a vacation

IT'S ALL ABOUT THE EGO

Manifest Destiny was thought of as a kind of *fate*. This is true in a sense, except that it wasn't a *natural* fate. It was the fate of the ego living out the consequences of its worldview. It wasn't an isolated period of history within one country. It was a global movement that began 6,000 years ago and continues today.

Manifest Destiny justified itself with the rationale "you can't stand in the way of progress." Of course, *progress* was defined by our paradigm—the paradigm based on the idea that humanity is separate from and superior to the rest of life. In other words, the *ego's* idea of progress.

Essentially, war is a clash between egos. War consists of two expanding boundaries that meet each other and refuse to back down. In the traditional image of war, the boundaries clash along the "front line"—the thin strip of battlefield between two versions of *us*. This remains essentially true, although the traditional image of war is becoming less common as the world becomes more complicated. The boundaries are less clear. The enemies are more diffuse. The means of battle are less direct.

It's all about greed. Nowadays, we're not supposed to mention that. But back in the "good old days" (like the Roman Empire) people were honest about it. "We're going to attack Africa to take their stuff!" said the leaders, and the people responded, "Yay!"

Nowadays, we tell ourselves that our wars are about things like "fighting terrorism." But perhaps you've noticed that we tend to fight terrorism in the exact locations where there are also resources (such as oil) that we want. Perhaps you've noticed that we don't tend to get as involved in fighting terrorism in the locations where there *aren't* resources (such as oil) that we want.

We also tell ourselves that our wars are about "advancing freedom and democracy." But based on a review of our recent military actions, such a justification only makes sense if interpret "fighting for freedom" as "fighting for the freedom of our corporations to dominate other economies." As for "fighting to advance democracy," my reply is: *Hahaha!* We barely have democracy ourselves. How about fighting to advance democracy in America?

Do you long for the "good old days"? I know that I do. I long for the president to give a press conference and explain the justification for our next war: "We're addicted to oil and they have oil so we're attacking them to get it." I mean, if we're going to kill, at least be honest about why we're doing it. I think we owe it to all the people who will become dead.

A WAR AGAINST MYSELF?

Our paradigm is at war against life. There are numerous problems with this, such as the fact that we're forms of life. We're expressions of nature. We're soil and seawater, all wrapped up into a living, breathing organism. Each of us is a veritable delight, a metabolic bundle of joy. We're living expressions of nature, dependent on nature for our physical survival. If we destroy nature, we destroy ourselves. Therefore, our war against nature—our war against life—is also a war against ourselves.

Wait, this sounds familiar. What was it that I wrote at the beginning of this chapter? It was something about how the members of the human race we label wise or enlightened refer to "the war within." Better take a deeper look at that, eh? *Maybe those folks that we label wise or enlightened are onto something.*

What do they mean by "the war within"? If we ask them, they reply with something about the "separate self" or the "skin-encapsulated ego." Ultimately we're all united—we're all expressions of the same thing. If we could get that darned ego out of the way, we'd realize this. We'd access the aspect of ourselves that's united with everything else. But to the extent we remain trapped in the ego, we retain a boundary that separates us from that aspect of ourselves. And separating ourselves from it puts us at war with it.

Ultimately the separate self, by its very nature, is in a state of war. Jiddu Krishnamurti wrote: "The whole structure of the 'me' is violence." The German philosopher Hegel went so far as to conclude that in every individual consciousness there's a fundamental hostility toward every other consciousness.

Those statements are somewhat extreme. As I see it, the severity of the war varies depending on how attached we are to our ego. Some of us are definitely experiencing "a war within," but most of us are only experiencing "an occasional skirmish within." Some of us contain a fundamental hostility toward every other consciousness, but most of us only contain a fundamental hostility toward the neighbor who runs their lawnmower Saturday at 7:00 a.m.

WAR IS HELL

We don't need to accept the religious conception of hell as an eternal afterlife of torment by heat and flames. We can understand such conceptions as metaphors for the kinds of psychological hells we experience during this life. Such as being tormented by the flames of self-destructive passions and the endless pursuit of selfish desires.

We can also think of hell as being trapped in addiction, of the hell of a life reduced to finding the next fix, of disregarding everything else in a continuing effort to sustain the addiction. We can also think of hell as being trapped in narcissism, of being trapped with a sense of inner insecurity that causes us to continually feel anxious, sensitive to rejection, and in constant need of validation.

As I see it, all these versions of hell are aspects of the same trap. As I see it, they're all symptoms of a disease whose cause is being trapped in the separate self.

LIFE IN HELL

If hell is to be trapped within the ego, what does that do to outer life? What is *hell on earth* or *life in hell*? There's the saying, "War is hell." That would be the extreme manifestation. That would be the ultimate result of two egos—two groups of egos with a common identity—taken to its ultimate conclusion. This definitely leads to the common conception of hell as unbearable suffering, as torment by flames and all the rest. Not metaphorically, but literally.

The consequence of remaining in the ego is to remain in "the war within." And remaining in that war results in fundamentalism, nationalism, and class conflict—all the factors in war listed earlier. It results in a mindset that wants "more" no matter the effects. It results in an economic system addicted to needing "more" no matter the effects. It results in steadily degrading the integrity of every ecosystem on earth, and using more natural resources than the planet can replenish.

Yet no matter how much we get, we're never satisfied. These distorted attempts fail to resolve the war within. And we're not happy about that! *Somebody's gotta pay!* Friedrich Nietzsche wrote, "Whoever is dissatisfied with himself is continually ready for revenge."

So on one hand, we want more stuff (greed). On the other hand, we need a scapegoat (revenge). And since human beings are so clever, we can figure out how to combine these two urges into one convenient package deal. It often includes nationalism ("We're number one and don't you forget it!") and religious fundamentalism ("Die you Devil-worshiping sons of bitches!"). Sooner or later, the perfect trigger comes along. And suddenly the *outer* or *economic* factors of war align with the *inner* or *psychological* factors. Greed aligns with revenge; the distorted pursuit of happiness aligns with the distorted purging of evil. And thus, *war!*

SUMMING UP

Here's my big philosophical conclusion to this whole train of thought: War is caused by greed, but greed is caused by another kind of war. "The war within" results in a mindset—a metaphysical foundation, a basic outlook on life—that arranges the physical aspects of society in a way that inexorably leads to "outer wars." The inner and outer factors in war complement each other perfectly.

A BIT OF HUMOR

Well, that got a bit "serious," didn't it. Let's add some levity. Here's Nietzsche's idea, expressed as a limerick:

I ♥ Scapegoating

Who'd have thought that my own private willing
Could result in such large-scale killing?
But millions of urges
For emotional purges
Makes news that's so strangely fulfilling

NOT A MISANTHROPE!

It could possibly be construed that I'm a *misanthrope*—a person who, upon seeing a human, says, "Eww! It's one of *those*." If that was construed, I must make it clear that such a construification would be incorrect. It would be *wrong wrong wrong!*

Certain misanthropes have considered the negative aspects of human history—the wars, the genocides, the ravaged ecosystems—and concluded that the entire human race is a disease. They consider the human species as intrinsically flawed—as an evolutionary mistake. And they look forward to the day when this flawed species finally eliminates itself.

I don't share this belief. I'm not looking forward to the day when this species finally eliminates itself. It's definitely happening. I'm just not looking forward to it.

Those nameless misanthropes have gone as far as to compare humanity with cancer—a disease that spreads uncontrollably and eventually destroys itself by destroying its host. Outrageous! Even though, technically speaking, humanity *is* spreading uncontrollably and is on the verge of destroying itself by destroying its host.

So the misanthropes kind of have a point. But how can we respond to the misanthropes and explain that even though we're acting like a disease we're not a disease?

WHAT'S A DISEASE?

To answer this question, we need some idea of what we mean by the word *disease*. This author defines *illness* as a response to a disruption to health, and *disease* as cause of the disruption. This definition is in agreement with our friend the dictionary, which defines disease as "an alteration of a living body that impairs its functioning" and "a disturbance, disruption, or cessation of normal functions of the body or its parts."

One aspect of disease is that the resulting illness draws a disproportionate amount of energy and resources from the host. German pathologist Rudolf Virchow stated this in what has become a basic maxim of medicine: "Every diseased part of the body holds a parasitic relationship to the rest of the healthy body to which it belongs, and lives at the expense of the organism."

WHAT'S THE WORST DISEASE?

Most people would say: *cancer.* Cancer inspires a degree of dread and fear deeper than other diseases. The underlying characteristic of cancer is unlimited growth. "Cancer cells," as one text summarizes, "divide without restraint, cross boundaries they were meant to respect, and fail to display the characteristics of the cell lineage from which they were derived."

Cancer cells are deviants. One aspect of what makes cancer such a sinister disease is because the deviance is from within. Cancer doesn't come from anywhere to invade us. Cancer cells arise from normal cells. Cancer consists of part of us—some of our own cells—becoming a renegade force turning against us.

It's an utterly irrational disease. It comes from nowhere and goes nowhere, killing itself as it kills the host on which it's utterly dependent. If it wins, it also loses.

SURELY HUMANITY ISN'T
LIKE THAT, IS IT?

From the perspective of life on earth, humanity definitely *acts* like a disease. If we think of humanity as "cells" in the collective body of earthly life, humanity is definitely "an alteration of a living body that impairs its functioning" and "a disturbance, disruption, or cessation of normal functions of the body or its parts." To paraphrase Rudolf Virchow, "Humanity holds a parasitic relationship to the rest of the healthy planet to which it belongs, and it lives at the expense of the organism."

But what's more disturbing are the parallels between our behavior and the processes of cancer. As with cancer, the underlying characteristic of our society is unlimited growth, most conspicuously demonstrated by an economic system addicted to growth. We've been taking an utterly irrational course, destroying the host on which we're utterly dependent. If we win, we also lose.

Does this mean the misanthropes are right?

OUR DISEASE

This author would like to propose that our disease is a certain *idea* adopted by humanity 6,000 years ago. It's a simple idea, which has become our core belief: *Humanity is separate from and superior to the rest of life.* Pathologists tell us that a tumor begins with what they call a "single ancestral cell." Our illness began with a "single ancestral idea" that eventually formed an entire cultural mindset.

The misanthropes are wrong. Humanity isn't a disease. Humanity *has* a disease. As a result of having this disease, humanity is experiencing an illness. The good news is that there's a cure. If the disease is separateness, then the cure is to end the separateness.

THE APOCALYPSE WON'T BE GOOD

To conclude this chapter, let's turn to the concept of *Armageddon*, commonly thought of as a kind of "ultimate war." I think of Armageddon as the endgame of greed. Stripped of its theological interpretations, Armageddon describes our war against life taken to its logical conclusion. In other words, our current course is leading us directly us to Armageddon. Not in a religious sense, but in a very real sense that will affect all of us, whether or not we go to church.

Christians see Armageddon coming, but they have a plan involving something called *The Rapture*. As I understand it, the idea is that as humanity is fighting with pointed sticks over the last scraps of food, the true believers will be whisked off to heaven.

When it doesn't happen, imagine those true believers in a state of shocked disbelief. Imagine their dismayed expressions— their tearful cries of "Why has my God forsaken me?"—as they discover themselves not whisked up to heaven, but stuck on earth fighting with pointed sticks along with the rest of us.

HOW CAN WE MAKE
ARMAGEDDON NOT HAPPEN?

To avoid it (Armageddon) is simple—in principle. All that needs to happen is for humanity to realize that life is an interconnected whole, and then re-structure every aspect of society to align with this realization. *Here comes the segue to the next chapter...*

Because if we don't, consider what will happen to our kids. What about future generations? What about the children?

CHAPTER 9

WHAT ABOUT
THE CHILDREN?

If you haven't figured it out yet, this author adheres to a philosophy of life based on life. It's a philosophy with the goal of making everything as life-affirming as possible—a philosophy with the guiding ethic of living in harmony with life.

With this in mind...

There's a prominent aspect of Christianity that's very relevant to such a philosophy. And there's no way I'm going to pass up the opportunity to comment on it, even though it will make me more reviled than I already am.

Surely there must be Christians concerned about the destruction of life. Wouldn't it be great if there was a Christian activist movement working in this area? It would be a movement that acknowledged that life contains a transcendent element—a dimension we may humbly define as *sacred*. And it would recognize that our highest ethical imperative is to honor and protect and nurture it. And it would take radical action to bear upon that in a very tangible way.

I think I'll do a Google search and see if I can find any Christian activist movements like this. I'll search for things like "Christians who support life" and "Christians for life." *Hold on a couple minutes, I'll let you know what I find.*

Okay... I'm starting to find some information...

Hmm...

Oh my goodness... This isn't what I expected at all!

Well, I don't quite know how to break it to you. I have good news and bad news. Believe it or not, I *did* find such a movement. It's called *Pro-Life*. But it's not what I imagined at all!

The good news is that it *does* acknowledge that life is sacred. And it *does* take radical action to bear upon that in a very tangible way. The bad news is that this "very tangible way" consists mostly of yelling at pregnant women.

Why yell at pregnant women? Well, because those women are considering not having their baby. And by yelling at them, maybe they can be convinced to affirm life by having the baby.

That's it? To be *Pro-Life* is to have a baby?

EVERYBODY GETS A TURN

Perhaps you Pro-Choice people are getting all smug and righteous. If so, don't worry. I'll get to you soon. Everybody will get their turn to revile this author.

DOES HAVING A BABY AFFIRM LIFE?

Consider the implications of having a baby. Specifically, an American baby. This author has run across several articles with titles such as "Having Children is One of the Most Destructive Things You Can Do to the Environment." According to one of those articles, having just one child results in an average of 102 tons of waste and 58.6 tons of CO_2-equivalent emissions per year. According to another article, an American family who chooses to have one fewer child would provide the same level of emissions reductions as 684 teenagers who choose to adopt comprehensive recycling for the rest of their lives.

So if you go ahead and have that baby, you've cancelled the life-long effects of 684 teenagers who are trying to save the planet. Not to guilt-trip you or anything, but those 684 teenagers will probably lose all hope and become drug addicts.

I'M PRO-BABY!

Don't get mad at me! I'm not anti-baby! In fact, I was once a baby myself. Some of my best friends were once babies. Babies are awesome! They're so—

Hold on, a bunch of Pro-Life activists are coming this way, and they look mad.

"We're mad!"

But what I just wrote are facts. You can't get mad at facts, can you?

"We're not mad at the facts."

You're not?

"No. We're mad at you for *telling us* the facts."

SPEAKING OF FACTS...

I've explored a variety of social and environmental problems in this book, but have yet to address the problem of *overpopulation*. It's a big problem that remains a taboo that few are willing to mention. I'm somewhat hesitant about mentioning it myself. It's a controversial subject.

Because a lot of people have babies. In fact some of my best friends who have babies have babies. If you're a parent of a baby that's reading this, *sorry!* If you're a baby that's reading this, that's pretty amazing.

But it's a fact that human civilization is unsustainable, and each increase of the human population is making human civilization increasingly unsustainable. What few people realize—or are willing to admit—is that having a baby increases the human population.

Yes, that's a very controversial statement. But I've never been one to shy away from radical views.

IN SEARCH OF SOLUTIONS

Let's say that, in America, we're destroying the capacity of the planet to sustain life by a factor of five. In other words, we're using resources five times faster than what's sustainable. If that seems a bit high, it's because America is much more unsustainable than the global average. If we want to be sustainable—and who doesn't?—we have a few options.

FIRST OPTION

If we want to create a sustainable world, and we're consuming resources five times faster than they can be replenished, we'd have to consume less by a factor of... *let's see...* (Sorry, my math skills are a bit rusty. Hold on while I grab my calculator.)

Okay, got it! We'd have to consume five times less. Okay, who wants to sign up for the first option?

sound of crickets

Apparently that option isn't terribly popular.

OPTION TWO

The second option is to reduce our population by a factor of five. In other words, reduce the human population to 20 percent of what it is now. Before you reject this idea immediately, consider that if we chose this option we wouldn't have to reduce our consumption at all! Follow along with your home calculators. If we're unsustainable by a factor of five, and if we reduce our population by a factor of five, then we can consume (on an individual basis) exactly as much as we're consuming right now! We can drive gas-guzzling cars! We can be wasteful with our water and other resources! We can be just as stupid as we are now!

Okay, who wants to sign up for option two?

sound of crickets

I'm surprised that this option isn't more popular. Usually, any option that allows us to stay stupid goes over very well. Apparently the desire to have babies is very strong.

So we need another option. We need an option that allows us to continue our unsustainable lifestyle *and* continue to have babies. Well, there *is* an option that would allow it, but I didn't want to bring it up before. It's pretty extreme.

OPTION THREE

The third option is to genetically alter ourselves to become really small, such as an inch tall. That way, even with our current population, we would use only a tiny fraction of our current resources. For example, cars for people an inch tall would get about 10,000 miles to the gallon. Homes for people an inch tall would use the amount of wood contained in a few twigs. A single potato would provide enough french fries for everyone in Dubuque, Iowa.

We could retain our current lifestyle *and* keep having babies. We wouldn't have to get smart. We'd only have to get *small*. What do y'all think of *that* option?

"We're not sure. We need to think about it for a while."

Well, here's one other thing to keep in mind. For those of you on diets, think of the weight you'd lose. Let's say you weigh 175 pounds. If we shrink you to one-inch tall, you'd weigh three ounces. And without needing to diet at all.

"Ooh, yeah! Sign us up for that option!"

Great! Unfortunately, we're not quite ready to proceed with that option—not until a few problems are worked out. Such as dealing with other forms of life that remained at their current size. For people one-inch tall, encountering a beetle would mean a life-or-death struggle. Family picnics would be ruined by crows swooping down to carry children back to their nest.

So option three, unfortunately, is not feasible unless we exterminate every form of life on this planet except for humanity.

We're working on this as hard as we can, but it might take a few years.

IN THE MEANTIME...

Let's consider some fun animal facts. Human animals generally refuse to reduce their population in response to environmental stress. But *other* animals do! At least, this author vaguely recalled hearing something like that somewhere.

To reinforce this author's vague memory, he was impelled to do actual research. Since Wikipedia didn't seem to have any relevant information, *this author was forced to search via other websites*.

People have no idea of the sacrifices authors make in order to satisfy their faithful and devoted readers. In this case, the author's sacrifice consisted of searching for information from scientific-type websites with articles that had long sentences and words that this author didn't understand.

According to an article about the effects of nutrition on reproduction, "Phosphorous and energy deficiencies are capable of preventing domestic animals from breeding successfully." Another article had a lot of useful information about wild deer. According to a study: "Nearly one-half of the does on inadequate diets failed to exhibit estrus." This author assumes that *estrus* is something that, if it doesn't happen, then neither do baby deer. Also: "Summer and fall nutrition is very important to fawn production. This was also shown with mule deer where the ovulation rate of does on depleted summer ranges was significantly reduced." This author is pretty sure that *ovulation* has something to do with reproduction. And finally: "Inadequate nutrition prevents mating of white-tailed deer." This author is reasonably confident that *mating* has something to do with reproduction.

Also, a more harsh method of what we might call "natural population control" occurs when nutritionally weakened deer (as well as other animals) are felled by predators.

For non-human animals, population control isn't a deliberate decision. But human animals like us need to reduce our population by choice and not as a result of being so skinny our bodies won't make babies or being so weakened that we can't defend ourselves from predators. We're able to use our incredible powers of self-conscious awareness to deduce with our large brains that we need to reduce our population.

Actually, there's a point at which "natural population control" will apply to human animals. It will eventually apply to us as a result of overriding earth's ability to support life to the point that our agricultural system collapses. But if we want to avoid such a harsh method, it's up to us to make the choice consciously.

FAITH IN LIFE = HAVE BABIES?

I may not have faith in humanity, but I have faith in life. Of course, to many people, "faith in life" translates to "faith in children."

This author doesn't really understand this reasoning. Consider that we're living on "deficit financing" in every possible way, bankrupting the environment and bankrupting the economy that's dependent on that environment. Rather than doing something about the situation, like *fixing* it, we have kids and set them loose while telling them, "Good luck, kid, you'll need it!" That's having faith in life?

BUT ONE OF OUR BABIES MIGHT BE THE ONE THAT SAVES THE WORLD

Is that a rational justification for having babies? Let's explore this question with a parent of an extremely cute baby.

Nice baby you got there! Hope it grows up before civilization collapses.

"You forgot to say how cute it is."

Oh yeah, it's a cute one for sure.

"Thanks! Don't worry about civilization collapsing, though, because one of our babies will figure out how to fix it."

You mean problems like environmental degradation?

"Yes, things like that. We don't know how to do it, but maybe one of our babies will."

And the overpopulation problem?

"That one, too. The more babies we have, the more chance we have of figuring out how to solve the overpopulation problem."

I'm pretty sure the solution to that problem is to have less babies.

"Well, that's for one of our babies to figure out."

But what if one of our babies doesn't figure it out?

"Well, maybe one of *their* babies will."

I WONDER WHAT YOUR
BABY WILL THINK OF THIS

What will your baby think when it grows up to realize you created it with the hopes that it might save our entire civilization? NO PRESSURE, HUH? That grown-up baby might not be too pleased with being put into this situation, and might ask why the parents didn't solve the problem of a collapsing civilization *before* bringing it into the world.

SELFISH?

In a rare instance of good news for the planet, an increasing number of people are deciding to not have babies. These people are observing the direction we're going, and deciding to not add another passenger to a sinking ship. These people have concluded that this is for the good of the passenger as well as for the good for the planet. Some of these people identify as *anti-*

natalist, a movement based on the tenet that it's cruel to bring sentient beings into the world if they're doomed to suffering and to causing suffering.

How noble!

But wait... There are many people who feel that this is *selfish*.

It's at this point that this author—normally a mild-mannered soul—starts to feel emotions that aren't what you would call *happy*. Because a lot of the people that feel this way—that believe *not* having a baby is selfish—have a lot of non-positive things to say about such selfish people.

I've run across several articles with titles such as, "Why So Many People Feel Outraged About Childfree Adults" and "The Real Reason Why Society Hates You If You Don't Have Kids." According to a study discussed in one of the articles, a substantial percentage of the population believes that people who don't have children are deserving of moral outrage. According to the participant of another study, "The only thing we hate more than a child-free person is a pregnant woman who is not happy about her pregnancy."

In response to this onslaught of screaming vindictive, I feel justified in composing a short quiz to see if the reader remembers some of the effects of having a baby (specifically, an American baby):

1. How many tons of waste will that baby produce?

2. How many tons of CO_2-equivalent emissions per year will that baby create?

3. As a result, how many teenagers will lose all hope and become drug addicts?

Answers:

1. *102*

2. *58.6*

3. *684*

Just to make sure I'm getting this straight, choosing to *not* do all this is selfish?

BABY = MEANING?

Of course, for many people having a baby is what gives their life meaning. It's how they take part in the grand scheme of life. It's their contribution to a process that started long before them, and will continue long after.

But if we don't have babies, what else could provide meaning in our lives? How could we possibly contribute to life if we don't have babies?

HOW ABOUT: LIFE = MEANING?

How about working to make civilization less destructive? How about helping to evolve civilization toward more life-affirming values? How about adding more truth and beauty to the world, since we're short on those. Or wisdom—we're definitely short on that. How about helping to make wisdom popular? I'm not sure how—maybe by printing up t-shirts that say "Wisdom is Sexy"?

Those are just a few ideas.

Perhaps there are some people who sincerely can't think of any ways they could contribute to life other than having a baby. For such people, there's no need to worry. Have a baby. Maybe when that baby grows up it will have some ideas.

DE-POPULATION IS A GREAT
IDEA IN ALMOST EVERY WAY

Economists and business people tell us that a growing population is necessary for economic growth. According to an article in *Bloomberg Businessweek*, "Population growth is vital for the world economy. It means more workers to build homes and produce goods, more consumers to buy things and spark innovation, and more citizens to pay taxes and attract trade."

As I'm sure you recall, economic growth is prominent on the list of things that we're addicted to. Since population growth is linked to economic growth, what would happen if the population shrank? According to an article in *Forbes* magazine, "For investors, the impact on asset prices could be striking. Competition and demand for natural resources such as water, minerals, and oil could wane, leading to deflationary pressure on commodity prices. Real estate prices and debt would also face similar situations."

Which means that the ability to profit would disappear, the real estate market would go into a downward spiral, and economic growth would stop. In other words, the economy would collapse and the zombies would eat our brains.

A PLAN

Okay, we need to regroup here. We definitely need to de-populate, but to do it in a way that the zombies don't eat our brains. What we need is a society that's sustainable, that will allow us to de-consume and de-populate without destroying the economy. We need to deliberately and consciously choose to create a society that's sustainable in every way—environmentally, socially, and economically. We need to choose a society that affirms life.

Hmm... Something about those two words... *choose... life.* Those words remind me of something...

ARE YOU PRO-LIFE
OR PRO-CHOICE?

Near the beginning of this chapter, I mentioned that the Pro-Choice people would get their turn. Now it's time for their turn.

Let's discuss the never-ending controversy between *Pro-Life* and *Pro-Choice*. For the record, my main issue with the Pro-Life movement is that it's *limited*. I'm not the first person to recognize that the movement seems to be preoccupied with the birth of the baby, and pays a lot less attention to the baby after it leaves the womb.

But my concerns go far beyond ensuring that the baby doesn't grow up a brothel that doubles as an opium den and has a meth lab in the basement. My concerns involve questions about the larger context in which the baby grows up. Does the entire culture support life? Is the civilization oriented to affirming life, to preserving the sacred in a way that extends to include life as a whole? These are questions that the Pro-Life people don't seem to be asking.

For the record, my main issue with the Pro-Choice movement is *also* that it's limited. Because the Pro-Choice people don't seem to be asking those questions either.

Consider the amazing ability of human choice. It's obviously much more extensive than the ability to choose whether to have a baby. We have the ability to consciously create any kind of society we want. What should we do we do with this amazing ability? What kind of civilization should be choose? How about *a civilization that affirms life?* Seen in this way, Pro-Choice and Pro-Life are complementary. The answer isn't one or the other, it's more of both.

HAVE LOTS OF BABIES!

Yes, this author has been putting forth arguments in favor of de-population. But considering what it would do to the economy, I have a new message: *Never mind.*

Keep having babies! Have lots of the cute little buggers. Because if you don't, the economy will collapse. And if the economy collapses, this author won't be able to have the nice little retirement he's looking forward to.

I suppose that might be considered to be selfish. Is this author selfish? *Naahhh.* How could hoping for people to have lots of babies possibly be selfish?

MAMA DON'T LET YOUR BABIES
GROW UP TO BE TODDLERS

The thing about babies is that they suddenly become children. It happens so fast, doesn't it? Very soon, they'll be the next generation of grown-ups. As for this generation of children, I'm very concerned for them. I'd be very concerned for my children, if I had children.

Did this author mention that he doesn't have children? Perhaps not, but it was pretty strongly implied by many statements made by this author.

Do you have children? Since I have spare concern that I'm not using, I'd be happy to be concerned for your children. My rates are very reasonable. How much are you willing to spend to have an actual book author be concerned for your children? You're probably thinking, "I can't afford it." But ask yourself: *Aren't your children worth it? Can you afford to NOT have an actual book author be concerned for your children?*

Children are a miracle. Every child is a unique product of the universe, a result of billions of years of evolution. Each person— each individual human consciousness—is an expression of universal consciousness. To experience a child is to experience that consciousness entering the world and searching for ways to become a meaningful part of it. In the words of poet Kahlil Gibran:

> Your children are not your children.
> They are the sons and daughters of Life's longing for itself.
> They come through you but not from you,
> And though they are with you yet they belong not to you.

When that miracle of human consciousness looks to us, we have a sacred duty to nurture the miracle of "life longing for itself." When we have a child, those innocent eyes look to us for guidance in understanding life, for guidance in how to succeed in life.

Consider the following conversation, which I was fortunate enough to overhear. It's a touching conversation between mother and daughter. I want to assure you, gentle reader, that despite my occasional "joking around" in this book, in matters such as this

I'm quite sincere. I want you to know that the following is an actual *fictional* conversation that really happened *in my mind*.

~ ~ ~

"Mommy, fourth grade is so boring! Why do I have to go to school anyway?"

"That's a very important question, honey! Let's play a little game, okay?"

"I like games!"

"Okay, repeat after me: *Would you like fries with that?*"

"I don't get it, mommy."

"That's what the people who work at Burger King say. They're working at what's called a *poverty-wage job*."

"What's that, mommy?"

"That's a job where no matter how hard you work you're always poor. Do you want to be poor and serve fries the rest of your life?"

"Why do people have to be poor, mommy?"

"Don't worry about that, honey. Get good grades in school so you can get into a good college. Then get good grades in college so you can get a job with a good salary. And then get good reviews at your job so you can get even better salaries. Then you can pay off the loan you needed to go to a good college."

"College costs money?"

"A *lot* of money! But if you get a good job that pays enough money to pay off the loan for college, then you can afford all kinds of other things. Such as our nice house. Do you know how much our nice house costs?"

"Hundreds of dollars?"

"Oh, honey, you make mommy laugh!"

"Did I make a joke?"

"Honey, our house costs *half a million dollars!*"

"Really? Wow! Why does a nice house cost so much?"

"Honey, that's just the way it is."

"I can't imagine that much money. The most I ever had was thirty dollars."

"Actually, our house will cost closer to a million, because of the interest on the loan."

"What's *interest*, mommy?"

"Well, the bank doesn't loan money for nothing, honey. So every month we have to pay them extra. This is why having a well-paying career is the most important thing. Also, every month you'll need to put some money into a retirement plan, so when you get old you won't be poor."

"Mommy, in school we learned about Social Security for when people stop working."

"Honey, Social Security is on the way out. It's slowing down the economy. Fortunately, I have a retirement plan at work."

"Will I have a retirement plan at work?"

"Probably not. Retirement plans are on the way out. They're slowing down the economy. So you'll need to put a lot of your own money into a retirement plan. And hope that the stock market doesn't collapse and wipe it all out."

"Mommy, I don't understand."

"That's okay, honey. The important thing is that you'll need to put money into the plan for your entire life. You'll also need money for a car. And also for food and clothes and fun things like movie tickets."

"Wow, I'm going to need a lot of money!"

"Do you understand now why it's so important to do well in school?"

"I sure do, mommy!"

"Not just *well*, but better than everyone else. Because you're competing against all the other kids."

"I am? Even against my friends Melissa and Alexis?"

"There aren't nearly enough good jobs to go around. If you don't become a winner and get a good job, you'll be a loser who's stuck with a bad job."

"You mean a job where you say *Do you want fries with that?*"

"Honey, you're so smart! That's a good sign you won't be a loser."

"But I don't want any of my friends to be losers! Why can't we all be winners?"

"Honey, some people have to lose or else the whole economy will collapse. That's just the way it is."

"I don't think anybody should have to lose."

"Honey, listen carefully because this is important. All good things come from the economy."

"Everything?"

"Everything that matters."

"Even sunshine?"

"Honey, I'm trying to be serious here."

"Sorry, mommy."

"It's really simple. If we serve the economy, the economy serves us."

"How do I do that?"

"By getting a good job, honey—just like I've been telling you all along. The most important thing is to make yourself look valuable to a company. You'll have to learn to think of yourself as a product. Have you put any thought into your brand?"

"My *what*?"

"Basically, you have to learn to sell yourself like any other product."

"Mommy, will my job be fun? Will I like it?"

"Honey, that's not important. The main thing is to attach yourself to a company with potential. Convince that company how much you care about them. Do whatever it takes to help your company succeed."

"Okay."

"But it's important to never forget that the company doesn't care about you."

"It doesn't?"

"It's nothing personal, honey. Employees are a company's biggest expense, and a company can only stay competitive by reducing expenses. So they're always looking for a way to eliminate your position, or figure out if it's cheaper to have someone in China do it."

"Mommy, I'm confused. I'm supposed to care about a company that wants to get rid of me?"

"Honey, you're so smart! You're going to do so well in the economy."

"I am?"

"And if you do really good at giving your life for the economy, then you can afford to buy all kinds of things to distract you."

"What kinds of things?"

"Oh, don't worry about that. There are lots of commercials and advertisements so you'll know exactly what you need."

"Like toys and things?"

"Well, the more grown-up you get, the more expensive the toys will be. But it's really important to buy lots of things, so you don't know that you're not happy."

"I'm not?"

"Well maybe you are now, but you won't be when you're a grown-up."

"I won't?"

"You'll totally lose track of the joy of being alive, if you haven't lost it already."

"Oh, I haven't lost it, mommy! Sometimes I'll notice colors and they're totally amazing! And sometimes I'll be super happy for no reason. I'll be so happy I think I'm going to explode in happiness, and it will be an explosion of rainbows and glitter. Mommy, do you remember feelings like that?"

"Just barely. When I see you experiencing those kinds of feelings it helps me to remember."

"Really?"

"Actually, no. The only way I can experience something even close to that is by getting drunk."

"I don't understand why people want to get drunk."

"Honey, you say that now. But just wait until you're a grown-up."

"I won't need to get drunk. If I want to be happy, I can watch my nature shows! I *love* nature! There are so many amazing animals. Under the ocean are things that look like they're from another planet."

"Honey, it's not a good idea to love nature too much."

"Why not, mommy?"

"If you love nature too much you'll be sad to see it destroyed. Wouldn't you rather go shopping?"

"Mommy, isn't it important to save nature? I learned in school that we depend on nature to live."

"Well, at school did they also tell you that saving nature slows down economic growth?"

"No, mommy, school didn't tell us that."

"Honey, school doesn't teach a lot of things. Schools are full of a lot of grown-ups who don't understand how the world works. It doesn't mean that they're bad people. They're just *ignorant.*"

"Mommy, in school I learned about *global warming* and *climate change.* Also, I heard about *peak oil.* Oil is running out and everything is going to get really bad."

"Oh honey, don't worry about that. There's plenty of oil left for this generation.

"But mommy, if we keep burning oil, global warming will get even worse."

"Don't worry about that honey. It's the next generation when it's going to get really bad."

"But mommy, *I'm* the next generation."

"Oh, sorry honey. I meant the next generation *after* you."

"But mommy, what if I have kids when I grow up?"

"Well, honey, I'm sure you'll love them just as much as I love you."

"But what about global warming and peak oil?"

"Honey, you can waste your time on questions like that. Or you can be practical."

"You mean like going to school and getting good grades?"

"Exactly! I want you to do very good in school and get a very good job and make lots of money."

"I love you too, mommy!"

To tell you the truth, gentle reader, this conversation isn't *totally* fictional. Some parts are based on actual conversations I've heard between parents and their children.

Do you understand why I don't have children? As I see it, if I had a child I'd have two options: Give my child the kind of advice as the mom in my semi-fictional conversation, or hope that my child has a fulfilling life eating from dumpsters. I don't like either of these options. For further insight as to why I don't have children, continue reading.

CHAPTER 10

CRISIS MANAGEMENT
ON A SINKING SHIP

Everybody knows the song "It's a Small World," right? It's the song played on the Disneyland ride of the same name. The ride is in the part of Disneyland called *Fantasyland*, which is an appropriate place for a ride portraying people from around the world that aren't shooting at each other.

For those of us not fortunate enough to have experienced the ride in person, just imagine boarding a little boat along with people from around the world—just like you're about to experience in the form of cute little animatronic puppets. There's a family visiting from Mexico. There's a couple visiting from Egypt.

You share a smile with your fellow passengers as the ride begins. You find yourself floating peacefully through scenes evoking cultures from around the world as those cute little animatronic puppets sing together in a spirit of global unity:

It's a world of laughter, a world of tears,
It's a world of hopes, and a world of fears;
There's so much that we share,
That it's time we're aware,
It's a small world after all.

But then the ride's over, and while getting off the boat the couple from Egypt yells at the Mexican family for getting in their way, and the Mexican family responds by pushing the couple from Egypt into the water.

Say goodbye to the *small world*. We're now back to living in a world full of egos. We're back to living in the *ego world*.

Let's embark together on an exploration of our descent toward inevitable collapse by updating Disney's heartwarming vision to make it a bit more relevant to our times:

It's a world out of touch with its real needs,
It's a world based on pursuing selfish greed;
There's one thing we all share,
We're all so unaware,
It's an ego world after all.

The remainder of this chapter explores how our decline is a consequence of living in a civilization based on an egotistical paradigm. Two expressions come to mind. The first is, "Pride goeth before a fall." The other is, "If you do not change direction, you may end up where you are heading."

WE'RE NOT BEING
IRRATIONAL ON PURPOSE

The term *arrested development* is usually applied to individuals. But it also applies to entire civilizations. We're collectively stuck on an ego-based worldview, and we're paying the price. But despite lots of flashing red lights telling us that this isn't working, we refuse to let go of that ego-based worldview. As a result, we're fighting to retain the assumptions that are causing our collapse.

This author is trying to make a very important point. So important that this author is going to put it in italics: *Human beings are not inherently irrational. It's the process of defending our paradigm in the face of glaring facts that makes us irrational, that makes us defend what's killing us.*

Defending our paradigm forces us to come up with increasingly ridiculous justifications for why peak oil isn't a problem, why global warming isn't important, why it's necessary to sacrifice the environment for the economy, why giving more money to the rich will help the poor *this* time, why we can't afford affordable housing, and why an economic system that must grow or collapse is sustainable.

In the final analysis, our irrational behavior is the result of refusing to enlarge the limited perspective of the human ego to something wider and more inclusive. We refuse to develop wisdom. We refuse to evolve. And to choose against evolution is to effectively go backwards as the effects of our irrationality catch up with us.

We don't have a precise term for this condition we've fallen victim to. There's not really a word for anti-wisdom, for the opposite of wisdom. There is, however, a word for the opposite of evolution: *de-evolution.*

WE ARE DEVO

Which brings us to consider *Devo*, the band whose overall philosophy was based on the concept of de-evolution.

In case you're not familiar with Devo, they're (according to Wikipedia) "an American rock band from Akron, Ohio formed in 1973. Devo is known for their music and stage shows mingling kitsch science fiction themes, deadpan surrealist humor, and mordantly satirical social commentary."

This author wants you to know that part of his extensive research prior to writing this chapter consisted of listening to Devo's first album, *Q: Are We Not Men? A: We Are Devo!* Based on this research, this author came to the following conclusion: *Damn! I'd forgotten what a great album that is!*

The concept of de-evolution originated in 1924 when Reverend B.H. Shadduck published his anti-evolution booklet *Jocko-Homo Heavenbound.* The term *Jocko-Homo* meant "ape-man." The booklet was a response to the unveiling of *The Chrysalis*, a sculpture portraying evolution by showing a man emerging from an ape "cocoon." (Later, the booklet would be referenced in the song "Jocko Homo" which introduced Devo's philosophy to the world.)

This was the era in which evolution was an extremely hot topic, just before the famous "Scopes Monkey Trial" in which the concept of biblical creation was pitted against Darwin's theory of evolution.

Of course, the concept of evolution, which is supported by overwhelming evidence, eventually became accepted. Except for a few holdouts who work to have the idea removed from school textbooks. Or to ensure that the idea is given equal status to the idea of *Creationism*, which is supported by no evidence at all. We might be tempted to accuse such people of being examples of de-evolution. But since they don't believe in evolution, it wouldn't be an insult; it would be a compliment.

Ironically, a funny thing happened just at the time when the concept of evolution—the idea that humanity was evolving toward higher potentials—was becoming accepted: *Evolution stopped working*. In fact, humanity seemed to be going back-wards.

The event that confirmed this for the founders of Devo was the Kent State shootings in 1970. For those of you who are unaware of this event, which was HUGE at the time, here's a summary. The Kent State shootings (according to Wikipedia) "were the shootings on May 4, 1970, of unarmed college students by members of the Ohio National Guard at Kent State University in Kent, Ohio, during a mass protest against the bombing of neutral Cambodia by United States military forces. Twenty-eight guardsmen fired approximately 67 rounds over a period of 13 seconds, killing four students and wounding nine others, one of whom suffered permanent paralysis."

In other words, unarmed students—demonstrating against a morally unjustifiable war that eventually would be recognized as unwinnable—were rewarded by being shot. Is it any wonder that some people at the time had the impression that humanity was not evolving toward higher potentials?

In 2018, Devo co-founder Gerald Casale reflected on Devo's legacy: "When Devo formed more than 40 years ago, we never dreamed that two decades into the 21st century, everything we had theorized would not only be proven, but also become worse than we had imagined." As for Devo's legacy for our impending collapse, "Today, Devo is merely the house band on the *Titanic*."

The concept of de-evolution isn't to be taken literally. It's not as if we're physically going back down the evolutionary continuum, although I've seen some people that make me wonder. De-evolution has to do with mental evolution, with the evolution of our ideas about the world. In all realms of life, the choice is *evolve or go extinct*. In the context of mental evolution, the choice is *evolve or get stupid*.

TIME TO STOCK UP ON CANNED GOODS AND RAZOR WIRE FENCE

Welcome to our era of *crisis management*. Get used to it, because it's going to define the remaining years of civilization. It's the most entertaining reality show you'll ever see, except it's not staged. It's 100 percent real, live on earth 24/7.

If aliens happen to visit us, they'll think it's the funniest show they've ever seen. They'll assume that all of us—the entire population of the earth—are members of an immense improvisational comedy group, performing a long-form routine (*very* long-form) based on the prompt "How can we exterminate ourselves?" Members of the group (us) will never break character, and if an alien comments, "Great show!" we'll reply, "What show?" The aliens will think this is *hilarious*.

THE DECLINE AND FALL OF OUR STANDARD OF LIVING

One of the most interesting aspects of the show, being performed right now, consists of the steady decline of consumerism in America. Not because Americans don't want it, but because Americans are increasingly unable to afford it. But even though it's declining, we're still pretty good at it. It's one of the few things at which America excels. Although the rest of the world is desperately trying to catch up with us, as far as consumerism goes we're currently *numero uno*.

¿Hablas español?

Hey, I just found out something really fun. While searching the symbol library for an upside-down question mark, I found a bunch of other cool symbols.

I wonder what ⅄ means. Same goes for ₾.

Here's a short love story: "Once upon a time ♀ met ♂ and fell in love."

Here's a more provocative version of that story: "Once upon a time ♀ met ♀ and fell in love."

This one looks like an apple: ☌

This one looks like a butt: (ω)

This one looks like an alien on a dance floor: Ж

Anyway... I was on the topic of consumerism. Consumerism was made possible by our war against life. And we were doing great while we were winning. But as a result of winning, now we're losing. We've reached the point where our war against life is making consumerism increasingly unaffordable.

Nobody seems to mention that a major cause of inflation is our war against life. Our unsustainable consumption is depleting resources, resulting in higher prices for pretty much everything. It's also causing higher prices due to shortages of things like eggs, as our addiction to antibiotics results in increases in drug-resistant diseases in the chickens that lay the eggs. Which often results in the need to kill millions of chickens. Sorry, chickens. If it's helpful, the livestock industry won't say you've been *slaughtered*, they'll say you were *depopulated*.

At the same time, our economy is plateauing as our economic growth addiction gets closer to bottoming out. Also, our addiction to rising housing prices means we have less disposable income. These dynamics are combining to put us into a sort of "permanent recession" in which a decline in real wages means we're increasingly unable to fulfil our vital patriotic duty of *shop till we drop*.

The emotional response to this is the opposite of satisfied. The emotional response to this is: *Let's band together at night and form an angry mob with torches.* The angry mob begins marching as it shouts, "Who took our consumerism away from us?"

The mob encounters some random person without a torch, who explains, "Well, our material standard of living, as well as the economic growth that made it possible, isn't sustainable. So we have to learn to adjust to the new reality of—"

"Burn the terrorist!" shouts the mob.

This works for a little while. The mob is satisfied while the terrorist is burning. But then—*oh oh!*—the terrorist is all burned up. Now what do we do? Who should we burn next? We're frustrated and afraid and we don't know who to burn. Perhaps our leaders can tell us?

ON THAT NOTE...

By this point, this author has set himself up to be reviled by pretty much everybody. Are there any groups of people left for this author to be reviled by? The answer is: *Yes!*

POLITICS: LEFT, RIGHT, OR FORWARD?

Let's begin our exploration of politics in a doomed society by introducing two new friends. We've had a lot of fun with our fundamentalist friends *Dogmatic Materialist* and *Dogmatic Religious Person*. Now, let's have some fun with our new fundamentalist friends *Dogmatic Democrat* and *Dogmatic Republican*.

A very wise person, whose name escapes me at the moment, wrote: "Denying half of political reality means that your views will be wrong half the time." To remain within their respective fundamentalisms, Republicans and Democrats must engage in defensive maneuvers to protect against information that contradicts their fundamentalisms. In response to facts that support their views, they smile and give a big "thumbs-up." On the other hand, when faced with facts that contradict their views, they yell and scream until they're blue in the face (if they're Democrats) or red in the face (if they're Republicans). As far as this author can determine, the two fundamentalisms go something like this:

Republicans: Yay for big business! Boo for big government! Capitalism will fix everything. Government can't be trusted.

Democrats: Yay for big government! Boo for unrestrained capitalism! The government will fix everything. Capitalism can't be trusted.

As a result, this is how the two fundamentalisms respond to different types of news stories. Regarding news stories about government corruption or incompetence:

Republicans give a rebel yell and shout, "We told you so!"

Democrats cover their ears and say, "La-la-la, we can't hear you."

However, regarding stories about corporate corruption or incompetence:

Democrats give a rebel yell and shout, "We told you so!"

Republicans cover their ears and say, "La-la-la, we can't hear you."

URPHHNGH

None of us like to face the possibility that we could be wrong—or even that our views are limited. There's a psychological term for this, for when our brain is faced with this horrible possibility. It's called *cognitive dissonance.* It consists of the experience when our brain goes URPHHNGH.

Let's consider a recent news story involving a woman who got kicked out of a Walmart for drinking wine out of a Pringles can.

Republicans might say, "Stupid moron, good thing she got kicked out." Or they might say, "What's wrong with that? I always drink wine out of a Pringles can."

Democrats have a problem. Their ideology holds that every person has equal worth and dignity, and that each person's ideas and opinions are just as valuable and important as everyone else's. As a result, they're not allowed to call people morons. So when millions of Democrats hear about a moron who got kicked out of a Walmart for drinking wine out of a Pringles can, you can hear—if you listen carefully—the sound of millions of Democrat brains going *URPHHNGH*.

Then those millions of Democrats turn to their copy of Barbara Ehrenreich's book *Nickel and Dimed: On (Not) Getting By in America*, reading feverishly for validation of their ideology that the noble working poor are doing the best they can to do right for themselves despite being held back by economic forces beyond their control. Thanks to Barbara Ehrenreich, they have a clear and unambiguous opinion of the working poor.

What about Republicans? Thanks to their fundamentalism, they also have a clear and unambiguous opinion of the working poor. It consists of: "Those morons are getting exactly what they deserve."

But wait...

What about that recent news story about the major corporation that went bankrupt and drained the employee pension plan while rewarding the top executives millions of dollars?

URPHHNGH.

That was the sounds of millions of Republican brains reading that story.

URPHHNGH.

That was the sounds of millions of Republican brains reading a news story about the companies they work for outsourcing millions of jobs to Indonesia

WHOOOSH.

That was the sound of those jobs rushing away.

Don't worry, Republicans, because now you can switch to being Democrats. Run out and grab a copy of *Nickel and Dimed: On (Not) Getting By in America*. If you're too poor to buy a copy, don't worry. Your liberal public library surely has a copy. Yes, you support public libraries now! They aren't socialism; they're a public resource. Public resources are good. We should raise taxes to pay for more of them.

What about Democrats? What could convert them to being born-again Republicans? There's a saying, "A conservative is a liberal who got mugged." So Democrats are doing just fine being Democrats, until that mugging. Or until the Pringles woman spills wine on their new Lexus. If that happens, don't worry, Democrats. Because the Republicans are waiting for you with their "tough on crime" policies. And as an added bonus, since you're no longer Democrats you're allowed to call people morons.

RATIONAL PEOPLE?

Conservatism and liberalism aren't directions. Conservatism and liberalism express a fundamental dichotomy of human nature: We exist as individuals yet also exist as a collective. Conservatism and liberalism embrace the two sides of that dichotomy to emphasize either the reality of our separateness or the reality of our unity. Conservatives are all about individual responsibility, and liberals are all about social responsibility. Conservatives are all about liberty, and liberals are all about justice.

Which is directly related to how the two sides view the role of government. Conservatives portray government as an intrusive presence that saps individual freedom. As opposed to liberals, who portray government as a helpful force that frees individuals from oppression.

Here's a crazy idea: Government can be either of these. It can even be both at the same time. But it's hard to see that if you remain stuck on one side of the dichotomy.

For rational people, it's clear that—

Sorry, there are no rational people left. Let's try again.

Back when there were a few rational people left, it was clear to them that the two sides are not opposites, but compliments. They're two aspects of human nature that have no fixed resolution. If either side "won" the result would be a dystopian society. So our task is an ongoing attempt at balance, with the strengths of each side compensating for the weaknesses of the other.

If liberals create problems as a result of being too "nice" (permissive, idealistic) it's up to conservatives to step in and be more "strict" (tough, practical). And vice-versa. Kind of like a stereotypical mom and dad from a 1950s sitcom, such as *Leave It to Beaver*. For those of you unfamiliar with the show, it was about a suburban family headed by Ward and June Cleaver, and starring child actor Jerry Mathers as Theodore Cleaver, nicknamed *The Beaver* for reasons that are never explained.

The political balancing act required by parents was illustrated perfectly in the episode "Way Too High." In that episode, June goes too far with the liberal approach and allows The Beaver to get wasted on vodka and leave the house, where he steals the family car and drives it into a telephone pole. As punishment, Ward wraps him in duct tape and locks him in the shed. But Ward went too far with the conservative approach, which he realizes when The Beaver escapes from the shed and attacks the family with a croquet mallet. At the end of the episode, balance is restored when June and Ward decide that The Beaver can get as wasted as he wants as long as he stays in his room.

That should be how the two-party system operates. But in America, the last time the two parties worked that way was around the time that *Leave It to Beaver* was being broadcast.

POLITICS AS A BROKEN BICYCLE

Ideally, the political balancing act is proceeding as civilization moves forward—as civilization evolves. But civilization isn't evolving. We're not even trying to evolve. We've lost any sense of positive direction. As a result, we've come to believe that left and right are directions. Since we have no idea what actual progress would consist of, we continue to confuse the question "Which way is America going?" with the question "Which side is winning?"

If we don't proceed in a forward direction, if we continue to think that "more government" or "less government" are directions, then the actual direction we proceed is *down*. I like to think of it as riding a bicycle. Left and right are ways you balance in order to go forward. But if you don't go forward, you fall. It's a perfect metaphor for our current condition: We're experiencing total political gridlock with two opposing sides focused solely on trying to bring the other side down, as we continue to base our civilization on the paradigm that's bringing us all down.

CORRUPTION ON TWO LEVELS

Our political system is corrupted by money on two levels. The obvious (superficial) level that many of us are aware of is the influence of money on government and the entire political process. The cost of mounting a successful election, especially for national office, has grown astronomically. As a result, politicians are almost totally dependent on large financial donations to get elected. Those inevitably come from large business interests. And of course, those who make the donations expect something in return. Sometimes it's for a vote on specific legislation favorable to the donor. But more generally, it's merely for actions favorable to business interests in general. Since politicians of both parties need the donations, this applies to both parties.

The deeper (more important) level that hardly anybody knows about is the addiction to economic growth. Even the politicians (very few) who don't fall prey to the obvious level have little choice but fall prey to the deeper level.

Because of this, our economy (and therefore our civilization) isn't based on satisfying the needs of Giuseppe the Fish Peddler (sorry, Giuseppe) but of major corporate and financial interests. Way back in the chapter about economics, this author explored how one result of the addiction is that the heroes of society are the entrepreneurs and business leaders who create growth. This has always been openly embraced by the Republican Party, which has traditionally held values consistent with business interests.

Yet the Democratic Party, which once upon a time (in a galaxy far, far away) was "the party of the people," eventually realized the need to worship the same heroes. In textbooks of ancient history, you can read amazing stories of the Democratic Party standing up to business interests with the bizarre reasoning that the purpose of business is to serve society, and not vice-versa.

Now, the Democratic Party pretends to be "the party of the people" by occasionally standing up to business interests with gentle suggestions such as, "If you'd be willing to share a little bit of your vast wealth, it would be really nice of you."

CO-DEPENDENCY IN
THE POLITICAL REALM

The reason that the two political parties appear to be a bickering co-dependent couple is because the two political parties are a bickering co-dependent couple. How do we define a co-dependent couple? How about this: *Two parties who ceaselessly bicker in order to avoid confronting deeper issues.*

Because there are definitely some deeper issues that the two political parties refuse to confront. One of them, of course, is the need to feed the Money Pit Junkie Monster. Although, of course, they don't put it like that. They put it in ways such as "Keeping America strong" (positive spin) or "Keeping America from collapsing" (negative spin).

Financial deregulation has proceeded steadily regardless of which political party was in power. The Republican administration of President Ronald Reagan began the deregulation of Wall Street in the 1980s. But it was continued by Democratic administrations, such as when President Bill Clinton signed the repeal of the Glass-Steagall Act, a key banking regulation, and approved the deregulation of derivatives with the Commodities Futures Modernization Act.

This resulted in the 2007-2008 financial collapse, which you might remember, and the subsequent bank bailouts which you also might remember. All of this had the support of both parties because our addiction to economic growth holds both parties hostage.

What if we threw out both parties? Sorry, it wouldn't make a difference, because if a new political party gained control it would also be held hostage.

The two political parties *are* capable of bipartisan co-operation. They worked together in harmony while singing "Kumbaya" as they did things such as authorizing $6 trillion for wars in Iraq and Afghanistan, $12.8 trillion for Wall Street bailouts, $37.5 billion per year to subsidize oil companies, and $1.5 trillion for the F35 military aircraft project. There are many more things that the two parties cooperated to waste our money on, but for the sake of those with high blood pressure let's stop here.

PRIMARY AND SECONDARY
CONSTITUENTS

Politicians have two sets of constituents: They need the public for votes to get elected, and they need big business for the growth that keeps the economy from collapsing. Politicians need to appeal to these two sets of constituents who—to put it mildly—don't always have common interests.

This puts politicians in an awkward situation. They need to tell the public that they're working to resolve our problems. But they can't admit how their support of big business to sustain our addiction to economic growth is causing those problems. As a result, both parties are led to propose solutions that consist of two opposite ways to not touch the source of our problems.

Let's consider how the parties respond to the problem of poverty. When Democrats talk about helping the poor, this inevitably means distributing money to people on the bottom with money obtained by raising taxes—the universal Democratic solution to every problem. How do we generate that money so it can be distributed to people on the bottom? How about *more economic growth?* Republicans propose to help the poor by adding money to the top so it can trickle down to the bottom—the universal Republican solution to every problem. How do we generate that money so it can be added to the top? How about *more economic growth?*

Unfortunately, both sides refuse to consider the fact that economic growth depends on poverty.

This also applies to the problem of unemployment, which economic growth also depends on. How do the parties respond to *that* problem? The Democratic solution is to promote educational opportunities. But they refuse to consider that although this helps some people to find jobs, the need for unemployment means that other people will be unable to find jobs. The Republican solution is tax breaks for business. But they refuse to consider all the studies that make it clear that this has almost no effect on unemployment.

A SWING TO THE EGO

Democrats are in an especially awkward situation. They're extremely limited in the extent to which they can demonize corporate CEOs and financial magnates as greedy misanthropes bankrupting poor Americans so they can buy more mansions. This is why—as you may have noticed—the Democratic Party has become much less outraged at examples of corporate corruption and incompetence, and is getting better at lip-synching old speeches by Ronald Reagan.

Democratic politicians might be dismayed at how they've been abandoned by the working class, but from the perspective of the working class the Democratic Party abandoned *them*. Which made it relatively easy for the Republican Party to rush into the void and claim *they're* "the party of the people," despite policies explicitly designed to enhance wealthy interests at the expense of the working class.

As a result, the political ground is shifting. The views held by President Eisenhower in the 1950s sound today like the views of a moderate Democrat. And today's liberals hold views similar to the views that conservatives held until around 1970. In other words, this country is on a political "swing to the right."

Or so the pundits claim. But do you want to know what's *really* happening? What's really happening is this: *We're on a swing to the ego.*

Allow me to explain.

We've based our civilization on an ego-based paradigm. As a result, everything's degrading. For a while, we could afford to spend our way out of our problems. But no more. The problems are getting worse, and one of the problems is that there's less money to fix the problems.

Solving the problems would require evolving beyond the ego and creating a life-affirming civilization. But this can't be considered, since the transition to sustainability would oppose a lifestyle based on the desires of the ego. As Vice President Dick Cheney said, "The American way of life is not negotiable." As a result, the problems continue to get worse. And we get desperate, trying harder to fix the problems with more of the same ego-based strategies that are causing the problems. And politically, the ones trying the hardest to push those ego-based strategies are from the right.

Republicans more fully embrace the paradigm that built America—the one that puts us at war with life. The Republicans aren't opposed to that war. In fact, they seem to actively promote it. The Republican environmental policy is to gut any regulations meant to preserve the environment. The current Republican energy policy consists of "Drill baby, drill!" in order to use up our remaining oil as quickly as possible. Yes, this will exacerbate global warming—which the Republicans solve by denying that it exists.

Conservative ideology has always been more supportive of the undeclared principles that America was founded upon—such as self-declared superiority that justified Manifest Destiny. This has led conservatives to embrace an extreme form of patriotism—a "Love it or leave it!" nationalism based on the unconditional acceptance of America as the greatest nation in the history of human civilization—a nation based on some noble values, but which advanced them with some less-than-noble actions. Such as genocide, slavery, colonialism, and imperialism.

In response to anybody who brings up the dark side of America—who is critical of America in any way—Republicans reply "You must hate America!"

Republicans are much better at appealing to the ego. They can't be beaten at that game. They'll wrap themselves in the flag (taking advantage of egotistical nationalism) and accuse all critics of any aspect of their program as *weak, soft, anti-American, anti-family, pro-terrorist, elitist, flag-burning, tofu-eating, espresso-sipping, tree-loving, people-hating, and God-denying.* By fully embracing the ego, anything the Democrats propose opposes the ego and is perceived as *sacrifice.* And egos don't like to sacrifice.

SLIGHTLY LESS EGOTISTICAL

But we can't let the Democrats off the hook. They like to pretend they're not egotistical. They like to present themselves as the party of caring and sharing. Yet for some reason they won't attack the Republicans for being egotistical. Why not?

The left won't attack the right's motives as egotistical because—brace yourself, are you sitting down?—*the left is only slightly less egotistical than the right.*

Democrats are uncomfortable with the kind of gung-ho "America Love It or Leave It" patriotism expressed by Republicans. But they're definitely comfortable with the results of that patriotism. Such as winning the wars that allow us to sustain the affluence that Democrats like just as much as Republicans. Democrats are slightly more willing to sacrifice than Republicans, who don't want to sacrifice at all. But how much are the Democrats willing to sacrifice?

Republicans refuse to admit that global warming exists. The Democrats—to their credit—acknowledge that global warming is real. As a result, some of them feel that it's important to drive less. Some of them might even choose to drive electric cars—while conveniently forgetting to mention what's involved in obtaining the lithium for the batteries and the rare earth minerals for the motors. Rather than bringing up those inconvenient truths, Democrats prefer to yell at Republicans for not doing anything at all.

Actually, some Republicans drive electric cars. But it's debatable whether this is because of concern for the environment, or because some of those electric cars look really cool.

THE AUTHOR'S OFFICIAL
POLITICAL POSITION

It should be obvious by this point that I don't identify as a member of either party. I don't identify as a member of *any* political party. The problem is that no party exists that aligns with my values. I would love to support the *Truth, Beauty, and Wisdom Party*, if it existed. I would settle for the *Avoiding the Collapse of Civilization Party*, but that doesn't exist either. I would definitely support the *Americans for Roller Skating Party*, which would ensure that all Americans have access to skating rinks for healthy life-affirming fun for the whole family.

Speaking of *fun*... I would lend my full support to a political party dedicated to maximizing fun, which would be called *The Party Party*. I'm not really an effective organizer, but maybe somebody out there would be willing to get this party started?

Just for the record, here's my official stance on the two major political parties: The Democrats frustrate me and the Republicans scare me.

WHAT THE HELL IS GOING ON
WITH THE REPUBLICAN PARTY?

Once upon a time (in a galaxy far, far away) the Republican Party represented conservative values. As a reminder (since it's been so long) those are things like, fiscal responsibility, limited government, small deficits, individual freedom, support of family and small businesses, respect for the Constitution, and maintaining an economic "level playing field" by which anybody can succeed. The Republican Party still claims to support such values, but if you examine what the Republicans are actually doing... Well, there's the expression: "Actions speak louder than words."

The Republican Party sold its soul by fully embracing the role of the Ego Party. They did this in 2020 during the Republican National Convention, when the Republican Party made history by putting forth no platform. Instead, the Republican Party officially became the party of the ego by announcing a "platform" that consisted of support for whatever President Donald Trump said or did.

Donald Trump was motivated by pure egotism, as we'll explore soon. And if the action taken at the 2020 Republican National Convention makes the Republican Party sound like a cult, that's also something we'll explore soon.

The Republican Party agenda is less about fixing our problems than about identifying scapegoats to blame for our problems. Immigrants are a very popular scapegoat. According to a 2015 poll, 75 percent of Republicans identified illegal immigration as the biggest challenge facing the country.

This is interesting. You might have expected other challenges to be more important, such as income disparity, racial injustice, gun violence, drug addiction, global warming, corporate influence on government policy, environmental degradation, the lack of affordable housing, rising health care costs, economic insecurity, and the elimination of gainful employment opportunities. But working on those other challenges would be hard. It's much easier to pass laws against immigrants.

FEAR!

Now we can return to our question of who we should burn next, after we burned up the terrorist who told us that our lifestyle wasn't sustainable.

Since neither political party is able to offer anything positive if they get elected, the campaigns of both sides consist mostly of fearmongering about how bad things will be if the other side gets elected. Both sides do this, but there's no denying that the Republicans have been much better at utilizing fear. We can trace this all the way back to that rascal Richard Nixon. He knew how to get elected, and it wasn't by appealing to wisdom, compassion, or self-sacrifice. "People react to fear, not to love," according to Tricky Dick.

This brings me to introduce research (stuff this author copied from a book) by long-time Republican John Dean. Yeah, he was kind of a "bad guy" for his role as the master manipulator of the Watergate break-in and subsequent cover-up. But he redeemed himself and became a "good guy" by becoming a key witness for the prosecution that eventually shut down Tricky Dick for good. So it's okay, he's cool now.

In his book *Conservatives Without Conscience*, he asks questions such as, "Why are right-wingers often malicious, mean-spirited, and disrespectful of even the basic codes of civility?" Asking questions which he goes on to answer, Dean employs a technique this author hopes to avoid. Why? Because it's obnoxious. Is it really? Yes, and it also sounds pretentious.

Ignoring the proclivities of this author, Dean forges ahead and concludes that Republican politicians use this strategy because fear encourages the desire for an authoritarian response, which Republicans are only too happy to provide.

As a result, what Dean calls the "politics of fear" has become a standard ploy: "They add a fear factor to every course of action they pursue."

FEAR VERSUS LOVE

The opposite of *fear*, as we all know, is *love*. Fear reinforces the ego; love requires us to move beyond the ego. Interestingly, there's one prominent example of a politician reacting against fear by embracing a message of love. This was Jimmy Carter, who actually used the word *love* in his campaign to win the presidency after Nixon was forced to resign due to the Watergate scandal.

Carter got away with it because Nixon had grown so corrupt that even many Republicans rejected him. And it didn't hurt that this occurred at the peak of post-war affluence, when America felt like it could afford at least a little love. Also, this was at a time—almost unbelievable to us now—that many Americans shared the idea that corruption is bad and should be punished, regardless of party affiliation.

Since then, things have gotten a lot worse in almost every way. Fear is on the increase, and the word *love* is only mentioned in connection with economic growth. And it has become impossible for a politician to be too corrupt, as long as they continue to appeal to the ego.

All of this leads us to consider the phenomenon of...

TRUMPISM

In 2015 frustration was rising and fear was running rampant. Continuing to utilize the "fear factor" that had been working so well for the Republican Party, Donald Trump seized upon the biggest fear of the Republican constituency.

We needed saving from immigrants, Trump told us, even though he was married to an immigrant, and even though everyone that's not a Native American is either an immigrant or descended from immigrants, and even though immigrants were—and are—indispensable to our economy for taking jobs that nobody else wants to do at wages that nobody else is willing to accept.

But such facts weren't a problem, because egos don't believe in facts. Facts don't matter. If a fact gets in the way of what the ego wants, the ego will deny it. If it can't be denied, the ego will declare that the fact isn't a fact. The ego will declare that it's "fake news."

As a result, our continuing "swing to the ego" led to the election of the most incompetent, corrupt, irresponsible, vindictive, divisive, self-centered president in American history—a serial liar who worked against democratic values, went to war against the media, and repeatedly defied the Constitution. He separated children from their families and put them in cages, mismanaged the COVID pandemic that killed nearly half a million Americans, suggested that people should inject bleach into their bodies to fight COVID, tear-gassed peaceful protesters so he could hold a photo-op holding a Bible in front of a church, got impeached twice, fired the FBI director for investigating his ties to Russia, called veterans and soldiers who died in combat "losers" and "suckers," coddled the leader of Saudi Arabia after he ordered the execution and dismembering of an American-based journalist, called neo-Nazis "very fine people," called Haiti and African nations "shithole" countries, repeatedly called the media "enemies of the people," violated the emoluments clause, praised dictators and authoritarians around the world while criticizing allies, falsely claimed that he won the 2016 popular vote, pressured the governor and secretary of state of Georgia to "find" him votes, and incited an insurrection against the government in an attempt to block the vote certification.

And despite all this, and much more—after clearly demonstrating such qualities for four years—this president came very close to being re-elected. And in a frightening development that threatens our future as a democracy, millions of people believe he *was* re-elected, despite the facts—which don't matter. And in another frightening development that threatens our future as a democracy, four years later America *really* re-elected him.

Many people couldn't understand why the public would vote for Trump despite being an authoritative narcissist bully. *No, no, no!* A lot of people voted for Trump *because* of being an authoritative narcissist bully. At certain times, for certain people, an authoritative narcissist bully is just what the doctor ordered.

Authoritative narcissist bullies don't exist in a vacuum. They exist in times of chaos. When things are going well, they get laughed off the stage. But what about in times of crisis? What about in times when people are confused and are looking for a savior? In that case, *bring on the authoritative narcissists bullies!*

TRUMP'S SUPERPOWER

Trump got away with things that no other president could have gotten away with. How could he get away with so openly and outrageously lying about everything on a continual basis? How could get away with being so brazenly corrupt? How could he get away with shamelessly breaking laws and defying the principles of the Constitution that he claimed to uphold?

The answer is that he got away with it all precisely *because* he did it so openly, outrageously, brazenly, and shamelessly. If he ever would have shown the least bit of self-doubt, remorse, or shame, it wouldn't have worked. Trump's superpower was egotism—open, outrageous, brazen, and shameless egotism.

How could people willingly allow themselves to be conned? How could people support a president who obviously didn't care about their needs, and advanced policies that explicitly worked against those needs? One reason it worked is that brazenness gives the impression of absolute confidence. It's interesting to note that the term *con man* is short for *confidence man*. It's the utter confidence of a con man that allows him to get away with the con.

A majority of Americans supported a president whose sole mission was a never-ending battle for ego gratification? That mission was so blatantly obvious that we can only conclude that his base supported him not *despite* it, but *because* of it. His base was attracted to the never-ending battle for ego-gratification because that was also their battle. Trump's egotism was his superpower because it appealed to others who wanted the same superpower. This is what drew the fervent devotion of his base. They were empowered by his egotism, as their egotism empowered his.

NARCISSISTIC COLLUSION

This leads us to consider the insights of psychologist Elizabeth Mika, a contributor to the book, *The Dangerous Case of Donald Trump*. She has written extensively about what she describes as *narcissistic collusion*,

> which describes the bond between a leader with Trump's character defect and his sycophants and followers. They mirror their imagined greatness to each other, and this mutually reinforced delusion of grandeur becomes an unshakable bond,

superseding any other considerations, like respect for truth and decency, or even a concern for one's reputation.

Trump fully understood the power of this bond. He said, "I could stand in the middle of 5th Avenue and shoot somebody and I wouldn't lose voters." Statements such as this caused people who study cults to realize that Trump's supporters were exhibiting classic cult-like behavior.

To further understand the phenomenon, this author was inspired—once again—to embark upon extensive research. But as happened previously, Wikipedia didn't provide what he was looking for. Once again, this author was forced to search via other websites. And on top of that, *this author was forced to utilize critical thinking skills in order to assess the information.* Honestly, this author can't take much more of this. This author is grateful that this book is nearly finished.

Your devoted yet mentally-exhausted author embarked upon a search for traits that cult leaders have in common. At or near the top of every list is *narcissism.* Well, I'd say we could give Trump a big √ for meeting this criteria, since a parade of psychologists (with their own marching band) diagnosed Trump as a pathological narcissist.

In case it isn't obvious, when we talk about *narcissism* we're basically talking about *egotism.* This is important to acknowledge, because it ties into the theme of this chapter, which this author is desperately attempting to conclude before his brain totally gives out.

The trait of narcissism (egotism) is directly (and rather logically) related to a constellation of other traits. And in a big surprise to nobody, Trump scored well on them all. *Sense of entitlement?* √ *Authoritarianism and lack of accountability?* √ *Refusal to accept criticism?* Definitely a big √ on that one. *Creates an "us versus them" mentality to deflect any perspectives that contradict their own?* Well, since Trump declared everything that contradicted his perspective as "fake news" I'd say he gets a √ for that one. That trait is directly related to another one: *Absolute certainty that they're right.* Since Trump has never admitted he was wrong about anything ever, we can give Trump a big $\sqrt{}$ for that one, too.

Here's another trait: Cult leaders tend to make *grandiose promises*, and the appeal of those promises are so powerful that the followers overlook any pesky factual evidence that the leader isn't fulfilling the promise.

How did Trump do on that one? *Well, let's see...* How about "Make America Great Again," a proposed return to a 1970s level of affluence that was only possible because of unique economic and historical circumstances that can never be repeated? I'd say Trump gets a $\sqrt{}$ for that one as well.

WHY JOIN A CULT?

The benefits of being a cult leader are somewhat obvious: devotion, adulation, power, money. But what about cult *members?* What's the source of the narcissistic collusion that blinds them to the ways in which they're being manipulated? What impels them to overlook the fact that the grandiose promises aren't working? Studies reveal that people who join cults share the following traits:

- a sense of disconnection, a feeling of being anonymous, rootless, or "adrift"

- low self-esteem, sometimes related to feeling like a "failure" according to social norms, sometimes related to feelings of shame

- extreme dislike of ambiguity, related to a strong need for security—a need for a simple answer that explains everything

Joining a cult resolves all of these problems by providing:

- an opportunity to belong to something greater than themselves

- enhanced self-worth as a result of that belonging

- one truth, one answer

Essentially, the traits of cult followers are problems that are consequences of being trapped in the ego. There's a right way to solve the problems, or course, which is to evolve—to expand the ego, to transcend the ego. But cults do something very clever. Since transcending the ego is hard (and we resist it with every fiber of our being) a cult gives the option of *giving up* the ego. Cult followers haven't transcended their egos to become one with something larger than themselves; they've surrendered their ego to become one with a bigger ego.

EGOTISM = FASCISM

Trump's fascist tendencies were impossible to ignore (except by his base, of course). It shouldn't be a surprise that our continuing "swing to the ego" is leading us to the type of political organization favored by authoritative narcissist bullies around the world throughout history.

The process of writing this chapter has led this author to the conclusion that fascism is the political expression of the negative aspects of the ego. Going down the list of those aspects, and comparing them with lists of the defining characteristics of fascism, they line up really well. Both lists include self-aggrandizement, the glorification of innate virtues, scapegoating, disregarding the rights of others, the worship of power and control, and the rejection of Enlightenment ideals.

And it shouldn't be a surprise that a central component of fascism is devotion to a cult leader. Fascism is characterized by a cult of personality toward a figure seen as an infallible redeeming force. Which perfectly describe the role played by Trump.

FRIENDLY FASCISM

Understanding the meaning of words is very important, according to people who sell dictionaries. It's also important for accurate understanding, according to whoever said: "Confusion in language leads to confusion in thought."

Actually, that was *me*. I said that. So according to people who sell dictionaries and me, when we start throwing around emotionally-loaded words like *fascism*, it's important to understand what the word really means.

We tend to associate fascism with a totalitarian state, a violent and overtly oppressive regime such as those of Italy and Germany in the 1930s and 1940s. In other words, a government that's definitely not friendly.

But it's important to realize that the original goal of fascism had nothing to do with a totalitarian state. The early 20th century Italians that invented fascism had a term for the concept: *estato corporativo*, or *the corporatist state*. According to the Italian leader Benito Mussolini, "Fascism should more properly be called corporatism because it is the merger of state and corporate power."

The common tendency is to associate fascism with an oppressive political system. But fascism doesn't need to exist under totalitarian rule. Because "the merger of state and corporate power" is the direction we've been heading in since the 1980s.

Yet this was happening while America was still officially a democracy. And it's getting worse while America is still officially a democracy. At least, it looks that way. The processes are still there, and every four years we're urged to vote. But from the 1980s onward, the candidates we're been given to choose from have largely been pre-selected, as are the choices they'll be required to make if elected.

In the 1980s, many felt that America had entered a new era of "post-democracy." *The New York Times* referred to it as an *overall corporate-government complex*. *The Wall Street Journal*, called it *benign totalitarianism*. Political philosopher Sheldon S. Wolin coined the term *inverted totalitarianism* to describe it. Unlike overt totalitarianism, inverted totalitarianism doesn't require a demagogue or charismatic leader; its power originates in the decentralized forces of the corporate state.

American social scientist Bertram Gross described it as *friendly fascism*. In the overt totalitarian fascist governments of the 1930s, industrialists and government officials sat side-by-side in the same planning agencies. This was an unprecedented situation at the time. But in America this became accepted as normal. Business interests increasingly dictating important policies, and in some cases wrote the policies themselves.

Most Americans were not unduly alarmed by this. They fully accepted the idea that America was becoming a corporate state, not realizing the concept of a "corporate state" is the very definition of fascism.

UNFRIENDLY FASCISM

Officially, America was founded upon the principles of democracy as stated in our founding documents. Yet America was also founded upon principles we weren't aware of—underlying assumptions that were so ingrained that we didn't consider them to be assumptions. But over time, as the implications of those assumptions played out, they eventually destroyed the stated principles.

Democracy has been unable to resolve our growing crisis. It hasn't been able to solve our problems because the source of our problems is deeper than democracy. But since democracy seems to be incapable of resolving our problems, a growing number of people are coming to the conclusion that democracy is the problem. Therefore, the solution is to get rid of democracy.

In theory, fascism doesn't require authoritarianism. But in it's obvious from history that, in practice, they go together. To the extent there's public resistance to fascism, authoritarianism is required to combat that resistance. Americans accepted *friendly fascism*, as long as things were going relatively well for most people. The problem now is that things are not going relatively well for most people. Which is why friendly fascism is getting less friendly.

The movement toward fascism was inevitable. If you base an entire civilization on the values of the ego, eventually things will degrade to the point when—after acting on those values destroys everything else—the last thing left is the ego fully revealed in its most fearful, desperate, and irrational form.

TRYING TO FIX THE PROBLEM
WITH MORE OF THE PROBLEM

In his rise to power, Donald Trump likely had no idea what he was doing. He just knew that being egotistical worked. Similarly, I doubt that the Republican Party deliberately set out to become the party of the ego, just as they didn't deliberately set out to create the conditions optimal for the rise of Donald Trump. But by deliberately becoming the party of fear it was inevitable.

Many prominent Republicans regretted the monster they created, but few were willing to share their regrets publicly in order to avoid the effects of the fear that they created. Meanwhile, a growing number of Republicans are copying Trump's strategy since they see how well it works.

For getting votes, that is. Not for solving our problems. Because it can't solve our problems. The idea that Trump's solutions could fix our problems was utterly misguided, since those "solutions" consisted of doubling-down on the causes. Trump arose in a time of chaos to save us with more of the strategies that caused the chaos. Trump was an egotist elected by a nation of egos to save us from the consequences of an ego-based lifestyle by reinforcing the ego. If we continue with our ego-based paradigm, Trump won't be the end of it. There will be more Trumps in our future.

GOING DOWN, TO THE TUNE OF "GUT
FEELING/(SLAP YOUR MAMMY)" FROM
Q: ARE WE NOT MEN? A: WE ARE DEVO!

Watch for increasing fear and decreasing rationality, because *fear trumps rationality*. It's like a game of rock-paper-scissors where rationality is always the scissors (sharp, incisive, good at cutting through lies and deception) and fear is always the rock (heavy, dull, good at smashing scissors). Thus, human civilization will go down, pounding itself in the head with a rock.

America is currently leading the way. But other countries are trying to catch up. Which is very strange. Why are other countries trying to catch up with a country that's going down? Nations around the world want an unsustainable standard of living just like us. And they're rapidly catching up. And if they catch up, that could be a problem. According to the latest figures, if the entire population of the earth had a standard of living equal to America, we would need six earths to provide the necessary resources. That could be a problem because our planet only has one earth.

Hmm... Sounds like we might be seeing some *conflicts* coming up in our short-term future.

Also, everybody else is engaged in the big economic pyramid scheme. Everybody else is engaged in the care and feeding of their own Money Pit Junkie Monster. Think of the economy as a huge bubble-effect phenomenon. Think of it as a big shiny soap bubble. Wow, it sure is pretty, with all the beautiful flowing rainbow colors. It's so pretty that we've forgotten that there's nothing supporting it, and that

eventually

bubbles

pop.

Chances are pretty good that no president will talk about this. Nobody wants this mess collapsing on *their* watch. So the official attitude toward this impending national disaster is: *Shhh... Don't mention it*.

From here on in, things will just get worse. And the worse things get, the more our stupidity will get us in deeper. Our responses to the disasters will be in the form of short-term crisis management—then as now—only they'll become more shrill and panicked. More scapegoats will need to be found, since we dealt with all the previous scapegoats and, *gosh darn it, the problems are still here*. Above all, we'll continue to orbit around the possibility that *we* could somehow have something to do with the mess.

This author will proceed to sum up this line of reasoning (capitalized and italicized because this author considers it to be important) as follows: *BY REFUSING TO RESOLVE THE ROOTS OF OUR PROBLEMS, WE'VE TRAPPED OURSELVES INTO PERPETUAL CRISIS MANAGEMENT. BUT WE DON'T REALIZE, AND REFUSE TO CONSIDER, THAT WE CREATED THE CRISIS.*

It's a vicious cycle going down, spinning faster the farther down it goes. Kind of like a toilet flushing. Which is an excellent metaphor for our condition. We're on board the *Titanic*, going down an immense toilet, with the house band Devo playing "Gut Feeling/(Slap Your Mammy)."

Which brings us back to the beginning of this chapter to revisit Disney's "Small World," and update it one last time:

Our collapsing world makes us want to frown.
And we don't understand why we're going down;
The one thing we exalt,
Is it can't be our fault,
It's a doomed world after all.

CONCLUSION

How to stop worrying and love humanity's self-destruction

If we consider our short-term future, things don't look good. On the bright side, there's no need to consider our long-term future because we don't have one. For some of us, this is troubling. How do we cope with the awareness that human civilization is taking a long walk on a short pier?

LET'S SAVE THE WORLD!

Here's an idea: We can engage in this thing called *activism* to make our civilization life-enhancing instead of life-destroying. I used to do quite a bit of activism. But not so much these days. My feelings align with those of an activist I knew many years ago, who wrote, "You feel like you're fighting a brushfire, and every time you stamp it out in one spot it just pops up somewhere else."

What do you do if you want to put out the underlying fire? As I see it, the battles are futile without changing the underlying paradigm which—if allowed to continue—will guarantee continual battles in a war that we'll eventually lose. To survive, humanity would have to recreate every aspect of civilization based on values that affirm life.

But since "humanity" is a collection of human individuals, this means the change would need to be made by human individuals. By people such as your neighbor. The one with the barking dog. Maybe if you can get your neighbor to acknowledge that their barking dog is a problem, you can get them to acknowledge that our paradigm is a problem. I hope you have better luck than me. Here's how my last conversation with the neighbor went:

Hi there, beautiful day isn't it.

"Sure is! What's on your mind?"

Just a little friendly neighborhood reminder that we need to be considerate of each other, such as keeping in mind that noise—

"What are you talking about?"

Well, maybe you're not aware that every afternoon your dog goes on a barking spree for about an hour and a half, and—

"If my dog's barking bothers you, then don't listen to it."

Well, it's really hard to not listen to, since your dog is very loud and barks really close to my window.

"Just play loud music that drowns out the barking."

But what I'm trying to do is relax in peace and quiet, not have a bunch of noise.

"If you want to listen to music that you think is noise, that's your problem."

Wouldn't it be much simpler to have your dog not bark so much?

"I don't tell you what kind of music to listen to, so you don't tell me what to do with my dog."

What are the chances that my neighbor is willing to examine the underlying assumptions of our civilization? What are the chances that *anybody's* neighbor is willing to examine the underlying assumptions of our civilization?

WHY ARE YOU TRYING TO
SAVE THESE PEOPLE?

Why work toward saving people like this? Why save a civilization full of people that accept the paradigm that's causing civilization to destroy itself? Because they'll just keep destroying civilization.

There's only one rationale for activism that makes sense to me: the idea that we can't change the paradigm directly, but by working against the various symptoms we're changing the paradigm indirectly. We're working from the periphery toward the center.

My three problems with this idea are: (1) there's not enough time, (2) we're barely making any progress on the symptoms, and (3) we're only working on some of the symptoms.

As for that last one, nobody at all is working on one of the biggest symptoms. Nobody is working to end our addiction to economic growth, which exacerbates all the other symptoms and—if not stopped—is enough by itself to take us down.

Humanity isn't intrinsically bad. We're just stuck on a silly idea. And if we don't care to examine it, then life will push us into looking at it. Actually, it's already happening. But so far, life has been pushing fairly gently. Life will be pushing us much harder in the future. At some point, life will start giving us bitch slaps.

Life only wants the *idea* to go extinct. Life only wants to separate a silly idea from the mind of one of its species. The problem is a faulty paradigm that humanity is attached to. And humanity refuses to get rid of it. So let natural selection do the job.

WHOA!

It's not like we *want* humanity to exterminate itself. But humanity is so determined to do so that if we get in their way we're labelled "domestic terrorists" and put in jail. So let's make it easier on everybody and get out of the way.

You don't like this idea? I believe doth protesteth too much.

Wait... Why am I talking like a Shakespearean actor with a lisp? And why is *lisp* the word for a condition that can't be pronounced by someone with the condition?

Once we've become able to separate ourselves—to watch humanity "from a distance"—this is what we can see: *Humanity is getting what's coming to them.* It's possible, with a bit of detachment and an inclination toward dark humor, to conclude that the number of people supporting their own self-destruction is precisely equal to the number of people that deserve it.

This was the message of Stanley Kubrick's classic 1964 movie *Dr. Strangelove. Or: How I Learned to Stop Worrying and Love the Bomb*, the genius of which I have honored by stealing the subtitle. By the end of the film, after having experienced human nature in all its glory, we're delighted to see Slim Pickens riding the bomb like a rodeo cowboy as he triggers the doomsday device that will destroy the human race. Our delight continues as we witness a montage of nuclear mushroom clouds accompanied by the 1939 recording of the song "We'll Meet Again" by Vera Lynn.

In case you're not aware of it, I should probably mention that *Dr. Strangelove* is a comedy—consistently ranked as one of the funniest films of all time.

A MOVIE ABOUT HUMANITY
DESTROYING ITSELF WITH
NUCLEAR WEAPONS IS A COMEDY?

Yes, and that's why it's so effective. The movie was just what the public needed in 1964 during the height of the cold war, when America's schoolchildren were taught to "duck and cover" as if getting under their desks would save them from a 10-megaton nuclear blast. The U.S.A. and the U.S.S.R. were engaged in an arms race, international tensions were high, and the 1962 Cuban Missile Crisis had led us to the brink of nuclear Armageddon. In 1964, Americans were ready for some stress relief.

One benefit of comedy is that it gives us the ability to laugh at things that might otherwise make us want to curl up in a ball and refuse to eat. Thus, *Dr. Strangelove*, a comedy about humanity destroying itself with nuclear weapons, was hugely popular. It gave people in 1964 the ability to laugh at the fact that, at any moment, they could be incinerated by a nuclear fireball. By the way, this is still the case. The situation hasn't changed at all. If this makes you ☹ I can recommend a movie that will make you ☺.

What's interesting is that the movie wasn't originally intended to be a comedy. It was intended to be a serious drama, based on the serious novel *Red Alert*. But an interesting thing happened when Kubrick began adapting it to film:

> My idea of doing it as a nightmare comedy came in the early weeks of working on the screenplay. I found that in trying to put meat on the bones and to imagine the scenes fully, one had to keep leaving out of it things which were either absurd or paradoxical, in order to keep it from being funny; and these things seemed to be close to the heart of the scenes in question.

The result was a continuous display of human absurdity. Such as the famous scene in the War Room, where the world's leaders are attacking each other, and the American president attempts to stop them by shouting, "No fighting in the War Room!" By the end of the film, it's not difficult to conclude that maybe it wouldn't be a bad thing if humanity goes extinct.

It's the same way I feel every time I see a politician arguing that we can't afford to end global warming. Just to be clear, what these politicians are arguing about is whether we can afford to not go extinct. And the problem isn't just politicians, of course, since those politicians were elected by a majority of the people who apparently agree with the reasoning that we can't afford to not go extinct.

DO PEOPLE REALLY
BELIEVE THAT IT'S OKAY
IF WE GO EXTINCT?

I recently ran across something that seems to suggest this. It was from a late-night television talk show—a "person on the street" segment where an interviewer sought the public's take on the hot topic of the day. The hot topic on this particular day was the news that one million species were going extinct due to human-caused climate change and habitat degradation.

The interviewer took to the streets of Los Angeles to ask the burning question: *Should Homo sapiens be saved from extinction?* That's us, of course. But many people were too stupid to know this. And one of the most fun things about people that are stupid is their enthusiasm in revealing it. My favorite answer was: "If they're going extinct that's very sad. But at the end of the day, I don't care." Well, that pretty much sums up my attitude as well. At the end of the day, I don't care either.

I can hear the arguments already. You might tell me something like, "If you're not a part of the solution, you're part of the problem." I would agree, but only if you can answer the question, "Where is the 'solution' that I can be part of? What group or organization is actively working on solving the roots of the problem?" When that group or organization exists, I'm *in*. Until then, how can I be part of a movement that doesn't exist?

The human tendency is to be dragged toward the truth in stages, kicking and screaming every step of the way, abandoning each level of self-deception after a life-or-death struggle in which each battle results in a loss of a tiny bit of our ignorance, leaving the rest to be ignored as long as humanly possible. *Forever* is our preference, if at all possible, thank you very much.

There's a joke that reveals a profound truth about human nature: "How many psychologists does it take to change a light bulb? Only one, but the light bulb has to want to change." To save itself, humanity has to want to change. But humanity doesn't even think it *has* to change.

So that's it for me. If y'all have your heart set on destroying yourselves, don't let me stop you. Just allow me to get out of the way of your crossfire before things start getting really nasty.

ACCEPTANCE BRINGS INNER PEACE

I should mention that I don't "love" humanity's self-destruction in the personal sense, just as (I'm assuming) Stanley Kubrick didn't "love" the bomb in the personal sense. I'm talking about love in the impersonal sense—in the sense of unconditional love, in the sense of total acceptance.

Humanity's self-destruction is only depressing if you remain emotionally attached. Depression is a sign that we need to let go of something. It's a sign that an obsolete idea needs to die. The idea that humanity has a chance of surviving is one of those ideas. Holding onto ideas that need to die isn't life-affirming. Therefore, to affirm life we need to let go of humanity.

Just to be clear, I'm not talking about *separation*. Because the meaning of life is all about realizing our fundamental unity, right? I'm talking about what Buddhism calls *nonattachment*. According to Buddhism, nonattachment is the opposite of separation. Attachment is based on the ego's attempt to defend against reality by attaching itself to illusions, and only by becoming free of illusions can we realize our fundamental unity.

If I haven't mentioned it before, Buddhism is a really great belief system to have at this point in history.

IS THIS AUTHOR SAYING
THAT WE SHOULD
JUST GIVE UP?

As for activism... Am I saying we should stop doing activism? Not at all. If activism is a meaningful part of your life, I wouldn't dream of recommending that you give it up. This author participates in modest forms of activism. This author also donates time and money to worthwhile causes. This author *does* have a conscience. This author sees all the destruction and injustice going on in the world, and couldn't imagine living with himself if he didn't contribute to making things better.

The trick is letting go of expectations. The activists I know that are too attached to expectations are the ones that get burned out. I've seen too many long-term activists whose activism-related frustration has taken over their lives. So this author takes part in activism, but has let go of expectations about the effects of that activism. I can't imagine any other way to carry on. There's too much disappointment otherwise.

HOW TO GET BACK
AT THE AUTHOR

Perhaps you're displeased with the author for his claim that we're doomed. If so, there's a way you can get back at the author: Get together with a bunch of other people who are also displeased with the author. Start a movement to create a life-affirming civilization. If you succeed, you can prove the author is wrong. Go ahead, prove me wrong. Please prove me wrong. *But just in case you can't prove the author is wrong...*

CONSIDER THE BIG PICTURE

Another aspect of Buddhism is to accept that nothing is permanent, that all things shall pass. Consider that life will continue to evolve once humanity is gone. Self-awareness will appear again in another form. Perhaps self-awareness will be evolved by dolphins, who are very clever and will probably survive our self-destruction. Some people consider dolphins to have already obtained self-awareness. Maybe so. Maybe the reason dolphins have that smile is because they're laughing at us.

Perhaps self-awareness will be evolved by badgers. As far as I know they're not very evolved, but the idea is fun to think about. Can you imagine self-aware badgers? Wouldn't that be something?

When self-awareness comes back next time, maybe the form of life that develops it will get it right. Maybe that form of life will examine the ruins of human civilization and be inspired to not follow our destructive path. If so, humanity can serve the role of "poster child" for what not to do.

YES, BARTENDER,
I'LL HAVE ANOTHER

Buddhism is one way of dealing with all of this. Another way is *Alcoholism*. These are two basic ways of dealing with troubling awareness: *Transcend it or smother it into oblivion*. They're two paths toward the same goal, broadly speaking. Through meditation, Buddhism encourages us to transcend our limited perspective. It seeks to transcend the past as well as the future in order to keep us focused on the "eternal present" Alcoholism, curiously enough, *also* seeks to keep us focused on the "eternal present." Not through meditation, but by getting so wasted that we forget the past and are incapable of considering the future.

This author doesn't recommend alcoholism. This author does, however, recommend *drinking*. Drinking is fun. It loosens us up at parties where we hardly know anyone. It helps us take ourselves less seriously. It makes us not care that other people can see us on the dance floor.

ANOTHER WAY TO DEAL
WITH ALL OF THIS

It's a way highly recommended by this author: *Comedy*. This author can't survive without comedy. Humor was an essential element of this book for the author, as he hopes it to be for the reader. As the movie *Dr. Strangelove* helped people cope with a situation that might otherwise make them want to curl up in a ball and refuse to eat, that's my hope for this book.

There's a saying: *Comedy is tragedy plus time*. There's another saying: *Comedy is tragedy that happens to someone else*. Both are different ways to say the same thing: Comedy is tragedy that you're not personally or emotionally invested in. Or in other words: *Comedy is tragedy that you're not attached to*.

We're back to *nonattachment*. That's the key.

As for the destruction of life on earth, this translates to: *I'm not part of the species that's doing this, therefore it must be another species.* If extraterrestrial beings arrive and ask me, "Hey, are you a member of the species that's destroying life on this planet?" my reply will be to point to humanity and say, "I believe you're looking for *them*." Then the extraterrestrial beings will say, "Thanks for your assistance. We're here from Interplanetary Pest Control. We heard there was a problem with a troublesome species on this planet. After we exterminate them, do you want to meet up with us for a beer?" I'll say, "Sure!" Then after we down some beers, I'll ask the extraterrestrial beings if they'd like to go roller skating, assuming they have feet that can fit into roller skates.

BREAKING UP IS HARD TO DO

It's never easy to end a relationship, even if our relationship is with a hopeless addict. But after they've broken promise after promise, we reach the point where we can't give them another chance. We know that giving them another chance isn't doing either of us any good. In hopes of helping you go through with this difficult process, I've composed a little speech you can deliver to humanity. Or write a letter and put it in an envelope addressed to *The Human Race, Earth, Solar System, Milky Way Galaxy, Universe.* I don't know the zip code offhand, but you can look it up.

> *Sorry, humanity. I wish I could say, "It's not about you, it's about me." But I can't. It's about you. As long as you refuse to end your addiction to destroying life, I have no choice. But I want you to know that it's been great, humanity. We've had some good times. I wish you the best and I hope you decide to not go extinct. Not just in hopes that you can win me back, but because it's best for you.*

Maybe if enough of us broke up with humanity it would make a difference? Maybe so, but I doubt it. After it sinks in that we're not coming back, humanity will just search for more co-dependent enablers. Unfortunately, there's an endless supply of gullible love-starved people willing to fall for those lines about how infinite growth is possible on a finite planet.

DON'T LET THE BASTARDS WIN

Perhaps you're asking yourself the following: *In the midst of a dying, life-defying culture hell-bent on self-destruction, how can I retain a positive attitude? How can I stay optimistic and happy?*

I have an answer!

It may sound counter-intuitive, but the best way to cope with a life-defying culture is to affirm life to the best of your abilities. In the big picture, we're doomed. So focus on the little picture. Focus on the differences you can make in your personal world. Add something life-enhancing to every moment. Make every interaction as life-affirming as possible. Leave every situation better than you found it. Add insight. Add humor. Add whatever the situation calls for to make it more alive, to make it a more genuine expression of life. If you allow humanity's downfall to destroy your capacity to affirm life, then the bastards have won. Don't let the bastards win.

SEIZE THE DAY

Things aren't too bad right now. But tomorrow will be worse. Which means that today is the best day we've got left. Which will also apply tomorrow. And to all subsequent tomorrows. So don't waste any time. Savor life while you can. Live every day to the fullest. In case nobody told you, we're surrounded by miracles all the time. Take the time to notice and appreciate them. We have an unfortunate tendency to take things for granted, to not realize what we've got until it's gone. Don't let that happen to you.

LET'S DANCE!

Rather than "doom and gloom," let's celebrate. Over time it will become harder to laugh, so let's laugh while we can. Let's party on the *Titanic* as it goes down. Isn't it true that the orchestra played on, even as the ship was sinking? And if the orchestra is playing, we might as well dance.

Care to dance? If you dance with me, I'll let you buy me a drink.

Hey... I think they're playing our song. It's the perfect song for humanity's self-destruction. We'll just sail into the sunset and... Oh, that's not a sunset. I guess it's the planet burning. Or maybe it's a nuclear fireball? I guess it doesn't really matter...

We'll meet again,
Don't know where,
Don't know when,
But I know we'll meet again
Some sunny day.

ABOUT THE AUTHOR

Scott Erickson is an award-winning writer of humor and satire. His humorous works include the novel *Icons Are People, Too*. His satirical works include the semi-fictional *The History of the Decline and Fall of America*.

He enjoys drinking beer and roller skating, but not at the same time. He is possibly the nicest curmudgeon you'll ever meet.

More information can be found at
www.scott-erickson-writer.com